the WORLD the FLESH & the DEVIL

the WORLD the FLESH & the DEVIL

by Harold Lindsell

SPECIAL CRUSADE EDITION

Published for the
Billy Graham Evangelistic Association

Published by
World Wide Publications
1313 Hennepin Avenue
Minneapolis, Minnesota 55403

BOOKS IN PRINT BY THE SAME AUTHOR

The Harper Study Bible
The Handbook of Christian Truth
(with Charles J. Woodbridge)
Missionary Principles and Practice
My Daily Quiet Time
When You Pray

ISBN # 0 913686 04 2
Copyright © 1973 by Canon Press
Washington, D.C.
Printed in the United States of America

TABLE OF CONTENTS

This book is dedicated

to my good friend and fellow Christian

William W. Clay who learned the hard way

that God answers prayer on the golf course.

PREFACE

Jean-Paul Sartre wrote: "Man can count on no one but himself; he is alone, abandoned on earth in the midst of his infinite responsibilities, without help, with no other aim than the one he sets himself, with no other destiny than the one he forges for himself on this earth."

Now if what Sartre said is true there is no need for a book like this; indeed it is reasonable to ask whether there is a need for any book by Sartre either. But what is more important is the idea expressed by this existentialist who believes that life is meaningless when he says that man has been "abandoned." To be abandoned is to be left to the mercy of someone or something. Implicit in his thought, whether he realizes it or not, is the idea that there must be someone or something greater than man who has abandoned man or left him to himself. Thus through the despair of this existentialist and his conclusion that man has no destiny other than what he makes for himself shines the defaced and marred image of God in man. And that is significant!

Against the backdrop of modern man's anguish we must paint the picture of God's incredible good news in Jesus Christ. Life does have meaning and man is not alone. Life does have purpose and design. There is help outside of himself and there is a destiny provided for him, if he chooses it, which is better than all his fancies and exceeds his fondest hopes and expectations.

This book is written primarily for people who believe in God and are committed to Jesus Christ for salvation made possible to them freely because of his death on the Cross. It is not a book which professes to have all the answers, but this does not mean that because we can't see everything that we can't see anything. We do see through a glass darkly, but this does not mean everything is invisible. And because we do not know everything about anything it does not mean we can say nothing about anything. There are some things about which we can be certain and there are others about which we can make tentative suggestions.

Basically this book concerns itself with the questions having to do with Christian conduct. But it can never be forgotten that what we do is dynamically related to what we believe. And what we believe is based on knowledge and faith. Knowledge without faith is sterile and faith without knowledge is absurdity. Therefore the matter of conduct is placed within the larger perspective of God's plan of the ages.

The reader is entitled to know the basic presuppositions that undergird the author's life and world view. I believe in God and hold that he has revealed himself to men in the Bible, the written Word of God. God is the creator of all things. Man was created with the power of contrary choice and through his voluntary act brought ruin to the human race. This was occasioned by the temptation which he did not resist and which was mediated to him through the activities of the malign creature we call the devil. Man was indeed in one sense abandoned by God and sentenced to death, but a loving God has made it possible for even abandoned man, whose destiny is hell, not heaven, to be reclaimed and restored so that what was lost in the first act of disobedience can be regained for eternity. This present world is the stage on which the drama of redemption is being acted out.

At the center of this redemption drama is a wooden Cross on which Jesus Christ hung and died outside the gates of Jerusalem. God deigned to become flesh and to live in human form. He lived a sinless life and through his sacrifice made it possible for sinful men to come back to their Creator. This God of redemption is the God of providence too. He is the sovereign God who works things out according to his plan, and his works and will cannot be thwarted. Someday his plan of the ages will be completed and the drama of history on this planet will have ended. The good will have triumphed and justice will have had its way. Wrong will be punished and right will be rewarded.

The world in which we live is a two-sided world. In it there are those who are in league with God and those who are in league with the devil. There are and can be no fence-sitters on this planet. Every man is committed to one power or the other. No one can serve two masters.

The Christian is a redeemed man who is called to serve the Redeemer. But he lives in a world shaped by conflict and is engaged in a life and death struggle. Pitted against the people of God are the devil and his angels, and the lost world of men. On the side of the saved is God who with Jesus the Son has given to his people the gift of the Holy Spirit, the third person of the Trinity. He indwells every believer, confirming in him the work of God and conforming him to the image of Jesus Christ.

It would be puerile to suggest that anyone should believe on Jesus Christ and all his troubles will be over. That is not only nonsense, it is contrary to the plain teachings of the Bible. The Christian life is a constant struggle, filled with hard situations and difficult decisions. It is a warfare that does not cease until death, but is also a life of challenge and filled with glorious possibilities. It is the proving ground of faith, the arena of spiritual battle, and the school of deepest learning.

The spirit of this age, even among Christians, is one that so frequently revolves around the subjective and caters to feelings. The great danger is to let the head follow the heart rather than the heart the head. If a man thinks right he will act right. If he thinks wrong he won't act right; indeed he can't act right. And that leads us to the question: how ought the Christian act in this world until Jesus Christ comes again?

The Christian faces three foes—the world, the flesh, and the devil. And these foes are not abstractions; they have concrete expression in specific matters of which we could give innumerable examples. These examples will be found in the discussions in this book having to do with Christian conduct. The list is not exhaustive nor the discussions and conclusions detailed. This work is more of a primer trying to open as many doors as possible, with the hope that the readers will search out other works that deal with some of the questions they are particularly interested in at length. This book tries to grapple with current problems, therefore its life will depend on the length of time these problems continue to vex and challenge people.

There are some questions that are timeless. There are others that are not. But even the timeless questions frequently require re-examination because wicked minds will always seek to destroy time-honored answers to these questions by attacking them from different angles and with more modern weapons. Some questions derive from purely cultural situations.

The answers to these may differ depending on the culture within which the question is posed. There are some things that may be right in one culture and wrong in another; these become questions of expediency, not of principle, and the ability to recognize what questions are matters of principle and what are matters of expedience is a delicate one demanding spiritual insight, a keen knowledge of the Bible, and the clear guidance of the Holy Spirit. Sometimes it is even as important to know *when* to do something as it is to know *what* to do.

The Christian always lives between the times: between the time of his conversion and the time of his consummation, which comes at death or the second advent of the Son of God. He lives between the time of his justification and the moment of his glorification. This period, as we shall see in due season, is known as the time of the believer's sanctification.

In deciding what the conduct of the Christian ought to be I have tried to base my judgments on the teachings of the Bible. I only ask that the reader consider my reasons seriously. And if he cannot be convinced, so much the worse for my presentation which is bound to be defective in part because I am finite. And if I have erred I can only plead that I did the best I could, expressed with integrity the viewpoint that I entertain, and cheerfully acknowledge that the reader has the liberty to test for himself my conclusions against Scripture, and accept or reject them with the understanding that each one of us must give account of himself before the judgment seat of Jesus Christ at the end of the age.

By interacting with one another we can sharpen our spiritual swords, increase our understanding, conform our conduct to the pattern of Scripture, and find a common ground of fellowship based upon our acceptance of the essential tenets of the Word of God.

I should express my appreciation to my children who have taught me as much or more than I have taught them. They have been perceptive and ready critics with keen eyes to detect my flaws and lay bare my hypocrisies. And now they have the privilege of repeating my mistakes with their own children and to decide afresh how close I have to come to living up to the principles I espouse in this volume. Words of appreciation to my wife of thirty years are wholly inadequate. What I am and have done are in no small measure due to her impact on my life. Every word I wrote has been salted with her personality and her thoughts. And to the host of God's people who have listened to me preach and teach and who have interacted with me in discussions on many of these important themes I can only say—Thank you.

INTRODUCTION

By Billy Graham

This is the book I had hoped an evangelical leader of Dr. Harold Lindsell's stature would write. It is incisive, bold and biblical. Not all evangelicals will agree with everything in it—but none can read THE WORLD, THE FLESH, AND THE DEVIL without being challenged as to our responsibility in discipleship.

"We hold," Paul wrote to Roman Christians, "that a man is justified by faith apart from works of law" (Rom. 3:28). But in another context, he calls for obedience: "Therefore, my beloved, as you have always obeyed, so now, not only as in my presence but much more in my absence, work out your own salvation with fear and trembling" (Phil. 2:12). Throughout its history, the true Church has guarded against two opposing errors: *legalism* and *antinomianism*.

It seems to me that there is an intimate relation between our *faith* and our *actions,* and it is important to see what it is. We are not justified by our behavior or by our actions; nor do they earn salvation or produce faith. But faith is not independent of action: it produces a pattern of acts, a life-style, that is consistent with itself. It is, in the words of the Authorized Version, "active in love" (Gal. 5:6).

Ethics, in a general sense, is the science of values, the study of good and evil. One may have a well-thought-out system; for example, he may subscribe to a particular school of ethics, such as Christian ethics, trying quite hard to live in accordance with it. Another may have no clear or comprehensive ethical structure on which he bases his conduct, but he too will make distinctions, perhaps only subconsciously, between right and wrong. There are certain actions that he will approve, others that he will condemn. In approving and condemning, one makes value judgments that presuppose a conscious or unconscious scale of values. Establishing a valid scale of values is the task of ethics. Biblical Christianity is not first and foremost a set of ethics, in the sense of proclaiming ethics as the way to God. It does not do that. But it does have significant ethical consequences, for God does not merely love us in a vague, generalized, formless way. He loves us with a purpose, and has a plan and a goal for us to achieve. Thus while ethics is not the cornerstone of biblical religion, neither is it just a decorative addition to it: it is part of the structure. It is not, like some college courses, "optional, for extra credit."

In recent decades, as culture has become more and more secularized, an attempt has been made to discard religiously based values in favor of more "objective" or "scientific" ones. But as the attempt has been made, and prolonged in spite of obvious setbacks, it has become increasingly evident that science, while it can frequently predict the consequences of certain choices, cannot tell you what you ought to choose. It cannot determine values.

In order to determine a set of values, it is necessary to make a kind of faith commitment consciously or unconsciously. It is possible to make a faith commitment to a philosophical world view, for example, such as Marxism, and its values. The founders of Marxism claimed to be *scientific* and *objective,* but it is evident that in fact, Marxism involves a system of values produced by a faith commitment to its principles, not through scientific investigation.

The biblical Christian, of course, has his reasons for rejecting philosophical theories as the source of values and turning to biblical revelation. This book is written primarily for people who have made this choice, who know themselves to be God's children through adoption in Jesus Christ, and who are looking for guidance in living accordingly. Dr. Lindsell has not written to evangelize or convert the non-Christian. If a non-Christian wants to know the reasons to become a Christian, he will find them here only by implication. But if he wants to know some of the practical aspects of *being* a Christian, this book should help him.

Writing for those who have accepted Jesus Christ as their "Teacher and Lord" (John 13:13), the author naturally follows his advice: "If you continue in my word, you are truly my disciples, and you will know the truth, and the truth will make you free" (John 8:31-32). Christian ethics is *prescriptive,* not *descriptive:* it is not a description of how individual Christians may be observed to act, but a prescription of the way in which their Lord wants them to act. As such, it necessarily is derived from the Word of God, which communicates his will and plan to us.

There are other books to explain *why* the Bible is authoritative, trustworthy, and the standard for life as well as faith. This book is addressed to those who believe in the Bible's authority, are willing to accept its standards, and want to see how these standards work out in daily living. It is not a book of philosophy or theology, *but a handbook for practical Christian living.* As such its down-to-earth, detailed counsel can be of invaluable help to the Christian, who knows that he already belongs to God but is confronted day by day with the challenges of living in a world that rebels against Him.

I. WORDS HAVE MEANING

"He's a liberal." "He's a conservative." "He's a radical." "He's a capitalist." "He's a socialist." "He's a reactionary." What do these words mean? To one person they mean one thing; to someone else they mean another. That's why we have dictionaries for defining terms.

But even with a dictionary handy, we all have our own ideas of what particular words mean. Often arguments and discussions bog down because we use the same words but unconsciously invest them with different meanings. When we do this we cannot talk intelligently because we are not on the same wavelength.

For the Christian one of the toughest word nuts to crack is *world*. This is true for two reasons. The first is that the word itself normally has a number of different definitions, so that one can be using it in a legitimate sense without really communicating to the person who is thinking of some other meaning. The second reason is that even when two of us are using the word in a similar context, each of us brings to the discussion his own peculiar bias based on many factors: cultural background, life style, hangups, theological convictions, and even age.

1

The place to begin is by defining ways to understand the word itself. Here the dictionary gets us off to a good start. *World* can mean:

1. The earth and the heavens and the universe, or all of creation.

2. The earth and the people who inhabit it, with all of their concerns; mankind or people in general.

3. A state of existence, a scene or sphere of life and action, as when we speak of the present world or the next world.

4. Those numbered among mankind who are engrossed in their concerns for this present life without regard for the possibility of the life to come. Christians usually think of these people as the unconverted or the ungodly part of mankind.

5. That which concerns the earth and its affairs as distinguished from heaven and its affairs; the concerns of this life as distinguished from those of the life to come.

6. The things of the world in the form of temporal possessions or worldly goods.

7. A certain class of persons, such as the world of science, the business world, the scholarly world, the musical world, and the political world.

You and I are part of the visible world in which all men live. We are familiar with our planet and know something about its geography. We would not be able to function easily in an environment unfamiliar to us in language and customs; but we do function well in our own situation, with our particular customs, economic system, and political heritage. In our own culture we differ from one another in physique, intelligence, psychological orientation, and freedom of choice. We are physical and spiritual beings who come into this world by birth, live for a short span of seventy or eighty years, and return to the earth from whence we came. The

Bible says we are dust and to dust we shall return (Gen. 3:19).

Life on this planet encompasses vegetable, animal, and human variations, all of which are interrelated and interdependent. Animal life depends on vegetable and other animal life for existence; vegetable life, in turn, depends on minerals, and all of these in their turn make human life possible. Without these interdependencies man would not be able to survive. But he does survive, and as a consequence the lower forms of life serve him.

Human life differs significantly from all other forms of life in two important ways: men have the faculty of reason and the power of choice. By thinking and choosing, men make their physical natures responsive to their mental and spiritual processes. They can communicate with one another through the gift of speech and thus share their thoughts. Thinking men ask themselves difficult questions, some of which they can answer; but there are many queries that can be answered only in part or not at all. This makes it clear that men are finite.

Man is naturally inquisitive. He sees the world about him, learns what happens and why it happens. But this knowledge, vast and important as it may be, leaves him with unanswered and possibly unanswerable questions. For example, we know man needs oxygen to live. We can trace what occurs when the body is deprived of oxygen by examining the blood, the lungs, and the respiratory processes. But one question remains for which there is no apparent answer: why is man a creature who needs oxygen in order to live? We do not know.

Man's knowledge continues to increase at a fantastic rate; yet the more he knows the more questions there are to be faced and answered. Indeed, the solution to one problem may open the door to many others. Amid the welter of questions and answers emerges an important fact. Most of the questions we seek to have answered, important as they appear to be at first sight, are not life's most urgent concerns. We could live quite successfully even if the answers to them continued to elude us.

Let us push all the lesser inquiries to one side. When we do this, four others appear to be basic and to constitute life's fundamental questions: 1. Who am I? 2. Where did I come from? 3. What am I here for? 4. Where am I going? Sages and scientists, young and old, male and female, have asked and tried to answer these from time immemorial. Immediately scores of related queries leap into my mind. For example, when I have asked, "Who am I?" I immediately wonder what the difference is between myself and animals. What is it that makes me what I am in my inner essence? Why am I unique from all other human beings? How is it that no two human beings are exactly alike physically, mentally, or emotionally?

My children have asked me the same question I asked my father: "Daddy, where did I come from?" Thinking children, as well as adults, are curious about the source of their existence. Is man only an animal? Have you and I developed in an accidental evolutionary fashion from ancient and lower forms of life? Did we indeed come from a first cell that originated in water; and from that first cell did all life have its origin, as some evolutionists tell us? Am I simply a higher form of animal? Is there a creator that made me? If so, why did he make me, what was *his* purpose, and why am I here? These and a hundred other questions leap through my mind and yours.

But the fourth question, "What happens to me after I die?" gives rise to others that must be answered beforehand. The first is whether there is in fact a life after death. Is there such a thing as immortality? Do people come back from the grave in some kind of resurrection? Is there some future existence marked by felicity and happiness which I have never fully found in this life? Is there some kind of judgment that differentiates the good from the bad? Is there a world to come? Is there any retribution for those like Adolf Hitler and Joseph Stalin, who did not act in a way man's sense of oughtness tells him they should have acted?

It does not take me long to discover that other people ask the same questions and answer them in different ways. It becomes clear that if I accept the answers given by some people, then the opposite answers must of necessity be untenable. If I believe that the grave is the end and there is no life after death, then it is irrational, if not stupid, to speak about a future life when there is none.

To whom or to what then shall I turn to get trustworthy and definitive answers to my ultimate questions? Shall I look to the scientist? Shall I look to the philosopher? Shall I look to myself? How am I to know that somebody else's answer is better or worse than my own? In my quest I learn that science and philosophy have limits to the questions that they can answer; in a dim fashion, however, I conclude that some answers can be perceived by the heart of man. For if man is only an animal who perishes forever when this life draws to a close, why have funeral services and mark off the grave with a tombstone? Why put flowers by way of remembrance on the grave of a corpse buried under six feet of sod? Animals do not build cities, take pictures of their loved ones, or place floral wreaths on tombstones. Why, if man is only an animal, does he do what no other animal does?

Although the heart does furnish man with some insights into the fundamental questions that he cannot get from either science or philosophy, there are nevertheless questions that the heart cannot answer. It cannot tell me who I really am, where I come from, or even define with accuracy what an upright man is. Therefore my questions require solutions from some other source. Here it is that God comes into the picture. He answers what science, philosophy or the heart cannot. He tells me who I am, where I come from, what I'm here for, and where I'm going. God has spoken and he has not stuttered in his speech. It is God who, in the Scriptures, has told men what they need to know, what they ought to know, and what they can know about the world and their relationship to it. This is important because we live in a particular age at a particular junction point in history, and sense how grave the problems are that we face.

This is an age of frightening contrasts, of much light and great darkness. We are threatened with a population explosion that makes it possible to forecast standing room only for man on this planet. We have ravaged nature by polluting the earth, turning rivers into cesspools, defiling the atmosphere with noxious gases, exploiting our resources, hastening the day when this globe will no longer be a fit place in which to live.

We must not overlook all of the good deeds men have done across the centuries, nor forget that some have lived exemplary lives, given themselves to the service of mankind, and worked selflessly for peace, brotherhood, and good will. But in an era marked more by evil than by good there are definite signs of increasing depravity and a worldwide turning away from good. Numerous and unending wars claim tens of thousands of people maimed or killed every year. Theft, adultery, fornication, lying, hate, envy, greed, pornography, materialism, force, and violence are commonplace. Man, who is thought to be higher than the animals, does things no animal would ever do. The jungles of Africa are safer than the streets of Washington and New York. Men lower than beasts will rob people and then murder them for the pleasure of seeing them die. This is our world in which we live and move and die.

Nowhere, even in the best of times, have the ideal goals of peace, progress, and plenty ever been approximated around the globe. The golden age longed for has never come; the good life envisioned by the finest minds and written about in a thousand books has somehow eluded mankind. Even those who claim to want a good world and a good life find they are at odds with themselves in their unwillingness to pay the price required to secure them; and those who are prepared to do so are prevented by the actions of the many.

So we find man, living out his few short years on the stage called the world. This world is the focus of our attention: the world of mountains, valleys, rivers, seas, and earth, populated by creatures called men, who are born, marry, procreate, and die—who think, talk, communicate, laugh, weep, work, sleep, eat, and wait for the summons that ends life's journey.

In our quest for answers to life's greatest questions we turn to that one place from which we can secure reliable information, to the Bible. The Holy Scriptures are the revelation of God to man. This book tells me who I am, where I come from, why I'm here, and where I'm going; it describes my relationship to the world and defines the different meanings of that word; it provides the answers that cannot be found anywhere else. This is the book then to which we must turn in a day of confusion, in a time of trouble, in an age of revolution and unrest, to find a roadmap that will lead us from where we are to where we ought to go. The answers are only as good as their source, which in this case is Almighty God himself. It is to him and to his revelation that we turn to find the answers to life's fundamental questions.

II. THE CREATOR AND THE REDEEMER

"It pleased God the Father, Son, and Holy Ghost, for the manifestation of the glory of his eternal power, wisdom, and goodness, in the beginning, to create, or make of nothing, the world and all things therein, whether visible or invisible, in the space of six days, and all very good." So reads the Westminster Confession of Faith, which bases its views of God the Creator on the teachings of the Bible, which it holds to be trustworthy and authoritative.

This raises a question about the relationship between science (biology, chemistry, physics) and faith in the area of creation. Many books have been written on this subject, and the end is not in sight. The purpose here is not to discuss this question in depth, but one or two observations will be helpful.

First, science cannot deal with the question of first causes. When it tries to, it has ceased being scientific and has entered the field of metaphysics (that branch of philosophy which deals with the nature and cause of being, and with the existence of God). As soon as the scientist says he is an atheist or a theist with regard to first causes, he has ceased being scientific. Science has limitations and cannot say where matter came from or that it always existed.

Second, science can and does postulate theories of how life began and developed; but these are theories and can never be ultimates. A case in point is the theory of general evolution. Some scientists think that all life sprang from a first cell that developed or came into being in water. Scientists who are Christians are divided about this. Some of them accept this postulate but believe that God was behind it all as the purposive agent. Others do not accept the theory of general evolution, believing rather that God was the immediate creator of each general form of life and ordained that it should reproduce after its own kind. The former are theistic evolutionists, the latter creationists.

We should note one fact. The scientist, whether an atheist, a theist, an evolutionist, or a creationist has left the realm of science and entered the realm of metaphysics, if he tries to answer the ultimate question of origins.

The Bible purports to answer what science cannot. Whether a Christian is a special creationist (which I am—but to which issue I will not address myself since it would require book length treatment) or a theistic evolutionist, he is so not because of science but because of biblical revelation. The Bible says flatly and repeatedly that God is the creator of the world, that from him all things spring; he made everything, seen and unseen, by the power of his word; he spoke and it was done. In him all things consist and hold together. "For in him all things were created, in heaven and on earth, visible and invisible, whether thrones or dominions or principalities or authorities—all things were created through him and for him" (Col. 1:16; see Rom. 11:36; 1 Cor. 8:6; Heb. 1:2; John 1:2, 3; Gen. 1:2; Rom. 1:20; Ps. 104:24; Jer. 10:12; Acts 17:24; Ex. 20:11; Gen. 1:31).

God's world is comprised of animate and inanimate things that reproduce themselves, and of those that do not. Inanimate objects such as metals, oil, gases, and liquids do not reproduce themselves. Animate objects like trees, birds, fish, animals and human beings do reproduce themselves. The animate and the inanimate are interrelated, however, and the continuance of human life is dependent upon both.

God the Creator of the world is also the author of natural laws. This assures men of order in creation, and supposes that what happens under a given set of circumstances, if repeated under the same circumstances, will yield the same result. On this basis depend medicine, farming, and almost all of the life processes. If tetracycline will cure one kind of disease, one can rightly assume that it will be effective in every case for the same disease. Apple seeds always produce apple trees, and orange trees invariably yield oranges. The union of the sexes reproduce their own kinds (despite lurid reports that some human beings have produced monkeys or vice versa). Miracles do not occur within the normal operation of the laws of nature, but are exceptions to them. Thus history knows of only one virgin birth, that of Jesus conceived in the womb of Mary; there have been a number of resurrections from the dead, but in view of the total number of people who have died the figure is infinitesimal (cf. 2 Kings 13:21; Matt. 27:52, 53; John 11:38-44). Although God is the author of natural laws, he is also greater than the laws he made and can and does supersede them when he so chooses.

When we ask, "*Why* does the world hold together?" we have to conclude as Christians that it does so simply and solely because God has ordained it. This determination is part of his overall plan for men, whom he has created and to whom he has given the earth as possession. If we ask, "*How* does it hold together?" we respond that here again the power of God is responsible. We do not fully understand all that has been disclosed by God's revelation of himself in Scripture.

The belief that God created and sustains the world by no

means precludes human efforts to probe the mysteries of life and creation, nor suggests that we should remain uncurious about such things. We are to think God's thoughts after him. He has invited us to unlock the mysteries of nature as best we can by research, and to probe for answers to basic questions. The more we learn, the more we realize there is to learn. And when we have found the answer to one question, we discover many new questions that we had not thought to ask before. Clearly man will never be able to learn everything, or always ask the right questions; indeed, he will never be fully able to ask *all* of the right questions.

The universe and the earth were pronounced by God to be good when he finished his creative work. Again and again the Bible says that God saw that his work was good (see Gen. 1:9, 12, 18, 21, 25). God's intention was that it should remain beautiful, ordered, and complete. In the beginning the world lacked some things that are commonplace now. There was no death, no sorrow, no tears. It was truly a paradise that would have met the highest expectations of any utopian, existing without blemish for God's glory and for man's good. God and man walked together in unbroken fellowship with nothing between them to impair that relationship, and there was nothing God did or would do to alter the relationship. If a change occurred, it would come about by something that man did, not God.

Into this paradise came the devil, Satan, and sin. Clearly sin and Satan existed first outside the world, but Scripture is not clear whether Satan sinned and fell before or after the creation of Adam and Eve. All we know for sure is that he did sin, that a multitude of angels fell with him, and that his fall had cosmic consequences involving the universe and the planet on which we live. Pride seems to have been at the heart of Satan's transgression. He wanted to be like the most high God (Ezek. 28:12 ff.; Isa. 14:12 ff.; Jude 6; 2 Pet. 2:4; 2 Cor. 11:4). He sought to wrest control of the universe, including the earth, from God. Satan had access to earth; and it was this malign spirit who, for reasons we are not told in Scripture, although the Book of Job may offer an answer,[1] was permitted to tempt our first parents, bringing about the fall of man with all of its disastrous consequences.

Of course we are faced with the mystery of why God permitted Satan to sin in the first place (the problem of God's sovereignty and his creatures' freedom of choice), and why, after he had sinned, he was permitted to tempt Adam and Eve. There is the even deeper mystery of how Jesus Christ can be the Lamb slain from the foundation of the world (Rev. 13:8). We try to resolve this problem by alluding to the omniscience of God; we affirm that he knows all things, even the end from the beginning, but we must at the same time assert that God is not the author of sin.

If we do not know exactly how sin came into the universe via the fall of Satan, we do know how sin came into the human race via Adam and Eve (Gen. 3:1-7). Any inability to understand completely how and why these things happened does not alter the facts in any essential sense. Man is what he is, and the real question is not how he got where he is but how can he be reclaimed from it.

The first man was a perfect being with moral responsibility and moral accountability. To him was given the power of choice. We need not belabor the age-old problem of free will in relation to salvation, but to say that in his sinless situation Adam was free and he was accountable. His choice in response to Satan's temptation, in which Eve connived, was to disobey God and eat of the fruit of the tree of the knowledge of good and evil. God had given him full freedom in the Garden except for this one prohibition as a test of his continuing obedience.

---

[1] cf. Job 1:6-12.

There was nothing in the Garden, in the covenant (see Gen. 1:28; 2:16, 17), or in the circumstances of his life that made it impossible for Adam not to sin. He was truly a free creature, linked to his God in a covenant that had for its seal his obedience in refraining to eat of the fruit of the tree. God warned him in advance of the consequences of disobedience—in the day that he should eat of that fruit he would surely die!

Compare the situation of Adam with that which exists today. We are told that man is a product of his environment: man is not sinful, he is sick and maladjusted; what happens isn't his fault, for he cannot help being what he is. The conclusion is that if man cannot help what happens, he is not responsible. Blame society and hold it accountable, but not the individual. Everywhere the Scripture emphasizes individual responsibility, declaring that he who performs the deed shall eat the fruit of it (see Ezek. 3:19; Rom. 14:12; Gal. 6:7).

Adam's transgression brought physical and spiritual death, as well as sin, to him and his posterity. The devil was the agent in Adam's fall, but Adam himself, and he alone, was responsible. His choice could not be, and was not, forced on him either by God or by Satan. As a result of the sins of Satan and Adam, the earth and the whole cosmos have been affected. Satan, the fallen angels, and man have joined forces against their creator and are linked together in the struggle.

One great difference distinguishes man from the fallen angels. They are not redeemable, whereas man is. Why the angels who lost their first estate can never be redeemed we are nowhere told. We are told, however, why man, who also lost his first estate, is redeemable. God freely of his own grace chose to do something about man's redemption. Perhaps this may be accounted for by the fact that the fall of

Adam differed from the fall of Satan in at least one important regard: no one solicited Satan to sin; his choice was made without the intervention or assistance of any tempter. Thus his guilt was greater and his condition remains unchanging. But Adam was solicited by Satan, who had already fallen, and thus Adam's transgression had in it a factor not present in Satan's fall.

The Bible proclaims that this is God's world, God's universe. He does not have and never did have any intention of surrendering his control to Satan permanently. Had he done so, God would not be God; Satan would himself be greater than the one who created him. From the beginning God had a plan, his plan of the ages, that would result at last in the downfall of the one who caused the chaos, and in the victory of the one who would be the redeemer. What is that plan and what does it envisage?

Man, by Adam's sin, was separated from God (Isa. 59:2). This separation included eternal death, which means no less than exclusion from the presence of God forever (2 Thess. 1:8,9). There was nothing man could do in and of himself to bridge the gap that separated him from God. Whatever could be done or was to be done had to spring from the person of God alone. The initiative had to be God's. He could conceivably have chosen not to redeem man. He could have permitted man to remain unredeemed and still have dealt with Satan; he could have allowed his cosmos to remain a ruin, his paradise never to be regained.

But God chose to redeem his lost creation, for he loved it (John 3:16). He chose to make possible the redemption of man as part of the divine plan (Eph. 2:8). At last the effects of sin in the universe were to be blotted out, the imperfections eliminated, the pristine beauty restored (2 Pet. 3:10-13). Great as the universe is, it is by no means as great as or greater than man made in the moral and spiritual image of God. God has provided for the redemption and the restoration of man as well as of the inanimate universe in which man has been enshrined (Rom. 8:18-23).

God will restore his lost creation, which included the universe apart from the earth, and the actual world in which men live. All of the inanimate creation will at last be redeemed and restored. But does this mean that everything in God's universe will be? Not at all. The fallen angels will never be redeemed. Whether this is because they forever spurn God or because their fall brought with it irremediable judgment makes little difference.

A portion of mankind will also remain unredeemed. The theologians have wrestled with this problem across the centuries. Some have concluded that God elects some to eternal life and condemns others to eternal death by divine fiat, or at least passes them over by his sovereign good pleasure.[2] Others have long held that man is a free agent and that whoever remains unredeemed does so because he chooses to spurn God's gracious offer of redemption and restoration.

---

[2] "Election" is a sovereign outworking of God's power to effect that which is pleasing to Him according to His righteous and holy will. The New Testament uses the term "elect" (*eklektoi*) to include a variety of meanings. Thus every believer is elected or chosen: (1) to good works (Eph. 2:10); (2) to conformity to the image of Christ (Rom. 8:29); (3) to eternal glory (Rom. 9:23); (4) to adoption as a son (Eph. 1:5). But the aspect of election which has given rise to dispute relates to salvation itself. It has been argued that if only those who are elected are saved, then the death of Christ was really intended only for them (limited atonement). Others insist that a "bona fide" offer to *all men everywhere to repent* (Acts 17:30) involves a divine intention for Christ's atonement to save all mankind (unlimited atonement). Scripture teaches that election is according to God's sovereign purpose (Rom. 9:11; Eph. 1:11) and that it is according to His foreknowledge (Rom. 8:29; 1 Pet. 1:2). But nowhere does the Bible make explicit what it is in God's foreknowledge that determines His elective choice. At all events, the Scriptures appear to teach clearly enough that men are free agents with moral responsibility, while at the same time God is sovereign and works out all things according to His own good pleasure. (Harper Study Bible, page 1748. Edited by H. Lindsell, Zondervan, 1962.)

Still others like to think that at last all men will be redeemed. Strangely, this kind of person is usually the one who passionately rejects the idea that God elects some to eternal life. But if all men are to be saved, then God must just as surely force into the kingdom those who do not wish to go. The universalist has an unlimited atonement, but he also has an election embracing all rather than some. However, the Scriptures do not support universalism, and we must conclude that there are men who at last, like Satan, will be cast into the lake of fire (Rev. 20:11-15).

God the Creator, in response to man's sin and the consequences which occasioned his separation, has become God the Redeemer (Isa. 41:14). He graciously extends to man the opportunity to be reconciled to himself (John 1:12). But the offer is on God's terms and by God's divine methodology. A sovereign God (Rom. 9:14-24) can do as he pleases, but a sovereign God who is a moral person operates in accord with his own attributes. God is holy (Lev. 11:44). The wages of sin is death (Rom. 6:23). Those wages must be paid out if sinful man and the world he lives in are to be brought back to God. Can man offer any payment that would be sufficient to take away the penalty and guilt of his own sin? Of course not. Eternal death is sin's wages. Man has no conceivable way of paying such a price to gain or merit eternal life (Titus 3:5). There has to be some other way, if there is a way, by which this can be accomplished; and it must be a way by which God remains a holy and a just God and at the same time is able to justify the wicked (Rom. 3:25, 26).

God's way of salvation is that he pay the price of sin himself (1 Pet. 2:24). This is a great mystery, but it remains a great truth. Whatever it was that had to be done, God had to do it. Salvation from sin begins and ends with God himself. He is the initiator, the one who carries it out, and the

16

one who completes it at last. This saving plan of God is manifested to man in two ways: through God's own self-revelation in the Scriptures, and in the incarnation of Jesus Christ, the Son of God and the Saviour of the world. Through the incarnation God himself became human flesh and sojourned among men. God himself identified with man's predicament, faced man's temptation, overcame man's disobedience, died in man's place, and rose from the grave to a life of victory over sin, death, and Satan.

God's purpose in coming into the world was to save sinners. His concern for men embraced all aspects of life, to be sure; but the most important purpose of all was the redemption and restoration of man to God. This involves being brought back into fellowship, being made members of the divine family, and being given the gift of everlasting life—all of which man had lost in the fall, and none of which could be recovered until sin's wages were paid, the justice of God was vindicated, and man's fallen nature had been renewed in holiness. What he lost in Adam man regained in Jesus Christ.

Jesus Christ came into the world to tell man and show him what the world really ought to be like. He elaborated the principles that should govern man's conduct, lived a perfect life of conformity to the will of his Father, and became a prototype of life for all; he brought heaven to earth, linked justice and mercy, emptied hell and populated heaven, took men from the clutch of Satan and brought them to the bosom of the Father. God's purpose for the world was salvation through grace. God's person who accomplished this was Jesus Christ his Son. Jesus' life, death, and resurrection were the perfection of God's outworked plan and never needed to be repeated. What the Father intended was fully accomplished and brought hope and deliverance to the human heart.

The earthly life of Jesus Christ, as important and necessary as it was, in itself was not enough. If all he did was become flesh, live a sinless life and then leave, the world would have been richer, but it would not have been redeemed. In order to restore God's lost creation, bring man back to fellowship with the Father, and end Satan's activity and dominion, something more than the mere physical presence of God on earth had to take place. Whatever needed to be done could not be done by man, but neither could it be done by Jesus living only in the flesh. Something more was required, something to do with the Cross of Calvary. That explains why our calendars divide time into the segments B.C. and A.D. (anno Domini—the year of our Lord)— before and after Christ. An event of cosmic significance for the world happened on the brow of that hill outside the gates of the city of Jerusalem; something that happened *in* history, an event that can be pinpointed as surely as any other, had reference also to things outside of history as we know it and beyond the scope of historical investigation and empirical evidence. Most certainly it dealt with the fourth of life's greatest questions, "Where do I go when this life on earth is over?" Had there been no Cross, even though Jesus lived on earth, there would be no hopeful answer to that question.

Let's acknowledge facts. Man's greatest problem has never been one of environment in the form of food, shelter, or clothing. It has never been that of human estrangement, racial strife or economic inequality. Man's greatest problem has been his alienation from God. He was made in God's image, rooted and grounded in God, and when man lost God he lost himself. But he is more than merely lost: he is "dead in trespasses and sins" (Eph. 2:1), having physical life but devoid of spiritual life. He does not have in him a deadly disease, but is already dead. This follows after the law of God—kind after its own kind. No child can inherit from his parents what they do not have. They can give physical life to their offspring but not spiritual life; and even the spiritual life they may obtain for themselves does not enter into the genes and the chromosomes. Each baby born into this world is born as his parents before him were born, estranged from God.

Man's problem is man. That problem exists because he is a sinner (Rom. 3:23). Children do not need to be taught to lie, cheat, and steal, but do so because it is consistent with their natures as sinners. They have to be taught not to do these things.

God's gracious response to man as a sinner is to extend to him the promise of deliverance from his sin, the hope of restoration to what he was before Adam's transgression in the Garden of Eden. Without divine deliverance man's life is limited to this world, and the only prospect in any life to come is eternal death. If man's greatest problem is sin, man's greatest enemy is death. Although he fears and seeks to conquer it, he knows with certainty that death comes to all. Fighting to prevent its taking place, he yields at last to its embrace. A sovereign God has appointed unto man a time to die (Heb. 9:27). This life is a life of probation, and willingly or unwillingly, man's probation ends, his life is seized, and his destiny is determined.

God's plan of the ages, centering in Jesus Christ and his death on the Cross as man's substitute, provides the only adequate answer to the question raised by death. God does not promise that his plan will eliminate death now, although that will be the case at last when the plan is finished and the final act of the drama has ended. But until that climactic event takes place, men everywhere, good and bad, must taste death. But *how* they taste death and *what* it signifies for them depends upon their relationship to Jesus Christ.

Those who approach death as Christians can be assured

of several things. First, the fear and dread of death need not be their lot. The sting of its permanence has been removed, and the sentence of everlasting separation from God has been revoked. The chains of captivity have been sundered; the prisoners have been set free. Old things have passed away. All things have become new.

Second, hope is provided of the better life to come. Death does not end all; a new and more excellent world lies before Christians, to which death is the doorway (Phil. 1:23). To be sure, those left behind will mourn. But to mourn for those who have died in Christ is misplaced sorrow. There should be rejoicing on their behalf because their pain is ended, their sorrow gone; a bright new world of perfection awaits them. Those who are left behind may sorrow for themselves and for their loss of the loved one, but they should rejoice in the good fortune of the one who has gone before them. Blessed indeed are those who die in the Lord (Rev. 14:13).

Third, man yearns for life, but it always eludes him outside of Christ. Every graveyard reminds him of the unceasing quest for immortality: tombstones, mausoleums, flowers, and markers all attest to man's urge to live forever. The Egyptian pyramids and the Valley of the Kings mark man's persistence; even the graffiti left by travelers on trees, benches, doors, and stones evidence this inward, perhaps even unconscious, desire to remain forever. Christ alone brings immortality, and for those who die in him he leaves his promises: "Because I live ye shall live also" (John 14:19); "I will prepare a place for you, that where I am there ye may be also (John 14:2). The Cross is God's answer to man's need; it has the effect of bringing life and light and immortality, implanting in the breast of every believer an unquenchable and an imperishable hope. Death for the Christian is only the beginning of a new and better life.

A word needs to be said about Christian hope in relation

to secular and/or Marxist hope. Christianity in its essence revolves around two foci: this present world and the world yet to come. While offering man hope both in this life and the future life, its major emphasis nevertheless is not on this life. Indeed, Scripture speaks of this world as transitory, perishable, and under the judgment of God; but the kingdom of God has entered into this dying world offering a final solution which is above and beyond history.

The secular and/or Marxist hope is concerned for this life only. The secularist hope (which need not be Marxist) and the Marxist hope share certain viewpoints in that both regard this world as all there is, assume the perfectibility of man and possibility of a perfect society, and look for justice and equality in the here and now. Those who take the developmental or evolutionary standpoint see mankind in a long, inexorable, but successful, climb from animality to a full blossomed humanity, all without God. The assumptions underlying these views are not from God's revelation, springing as they do from the mind and imagination of man. But they constitute articles of belief and thus have a "religiosity" about them that makes both secularism and Marxism a sort of religious faith.

Christian hope, however, is based on biblical presuppositions which declare that man is sinful, that society will never be perfected in this present evil and Satan-dominated world, and that man's best plans go astray. God is fashioning a better world, a perfect one in which sin will be dealt with and finally eliminated. Man's real hope in eternity, as measured against time, will be realized in and through Jesus Christ. Against this backdrop the secular and Marxist hope must be seen as unrealizable, inadequate, and fatally defective —unless there is no God, no salvation, and no future life. In that event, the most that secular and Marxist hope can offer is the possibility of an adequate material existence for man's normal span of life, minus the spiritual aspect which makes man human. And its absence is the final and fatal flaw that makes the Christian hope so totally different from these current substitutes.

God's plan of the ages has not yet been completed. Indeed, two thousand years have elapsed since Jesus came, died, and rose again. At times it appears that the end is no nearer than when he first rose. Some have mocked Christianity, asking bitingly, "Where is the promise of his coming?" (2 Pet. 3:4). The Christian himself, wholly apart from unbelievers, must ask himself, "When will Christ come, and why does he delay?" "Why doesn't God finish his plan, bring in his kingdom, wipe out Satan and sin, and restore the Paradise man lost in Adam?" There are a number of reasons why God's plan still remains uncompleted.

First, Christ died to redeem men yet unborn. God alone knows how long history must continue until the souls of all the redeemed have entered this world. But until they have, time will go on.

Second, God's plan was formulated in eternity but is executed in time. To God a thousand years are as one day (2 Pet. 3:8). Man's understanding of time differs from that of God, who works according to his own purposes and is never in a hurry. The Bible itself was written by many authors over approximately fifteen hundred years, before the canon of Scripture was closed. The Levitical priests offered their animal sacrifices year in and year out, for hundreds of years, before the one perfect and final sacrifice appeared. Daniel prophesied the time of the Redeemer's coming more than five hundred years before the actual event. God's pace from man's perspective sometimes appears leisurely.

Third, God has ordained that his plan will be completed only when the Gospel has been preached to every creature

(Matt. 24:14). He has entrusted this responsibility to his pilgrim people, and thus in some sense the completion of the plan is related to the labors of the saints. Angels cannot preach the Gospel, only men can. And until the Gospel is fully preached, the consummation cannot come. God alone knows when the Gospel will have been adequately preached and the terms of the Great Commission fulfilled, at which time Christ will come. But so long as he tarries, the task is not finished. The Church can hasten the coming of the Lord by taking the Gospel to every creature (2 Pet. 3:12).

Fourth, God's plan includes the fulfillment of prophecies that take time to work out. For example, Jesus prophesied the destruction of Jerusalem (Luke 21:20), an event which did not take place until A.D. 70, some decades after his resurrection. It did not occur immediately because time was required for the stage to be set. Jesus also said that Jerusalem would be under the domination of the Gentiles until the times of the Gentiles should be fulfilled (Luke 21:24). For nineteen hundred years this prophecy was not fulfilled. However, since 1967 the Jews have controlled Jerusalem. May not the times of the Gentiles referred to by Jesus in Luke's Gospel be coming to a close, evidenced by the fact that Jerusalem is in Jewish hands once again?

Many times during the past two thousand years men have mistakenly thought that the end of the age was upon them. The circumstances were often characteristic of the closing days of the final age described in Scripture. Probably the state of affairs will always be such that Christians can ask themselves, "Is not the coming of the Lord near?" Therefore they must always be cautious, remembering that other people in other ages lived through times just as difficult and just as troubled as those that distinguish this present era. Signs are easy to misread.

In this age of great anxiety men look back to earlier days

thinking conditions were so much better then, when in fact they may have been equally as bad or worse. For example, the Victorian Age in England is often regarded as one of prudish rectitude and stolid peacefulness, when in fact it was deeply marked by gross sins, sins often hidden from the people of that age. What was done secretly then, however, is done openly now.

Divorce is commonplace in today's culture, whereas it was relatively rare in the Victorian Age. But immorality was widespread then as now. In America President Franklin Delano Roosevelt's five children have accumulated fifteen divorces and remarriages among them. No outstanding Victorian family equalled that record, yet the age may have been worse in some ways. Gladstone, a prime minister of England, said he had known eleven former prime ministers every one of whom was an adulterer.

During this period more than one quarter of the people of England could not write their own names, and over half of them couldn't read. Almost fifty per cent of the children were not in school. Unwanted youngsters were given Godfrey's Cordial, made of opium, treacle and sassafras, for a quick and painless death. Children at ten years of age worked in factories six days a week; at twelve they were in the coal mines. At thirteen the white slave traffic threatened. Almost sixteen million English workers lived below the poverty line; three million white-collar people lived slightly above it. Servants slept in cellars without windows and in attics with no fresh air. London dockworkers struck for sixpence an hour more, and Matthew Arnold, essayist and poet, wrote that England was "on the verge of anarchy." [3]

God's plan of the ages has been fashioned to grapple with these problems—spiritual, personal, political, economic,

---

[3] See here the account by Ralph G. Marten, *Jennie,* the life of Lady Randolph Churchill, N.Y., 1969, pp. 46, 50, 174, 243, 257-8, 263.

and national. Each era has been different, and yet all have been the same. Sin is the root of the problems of every age, and has manifested itself in personal and social life in a myriad of forms. There never has been a golden age; all have been bad because the whole world lies in the grip of the evil one. But into every age God has come in redeeming power. His Gospel has always gripped the hearts of some men, for God's business is the calling out of a people for his name, a bride for his Bridegroom, sons and daughters for his kingdom.

If each age has had its sin and grossest sinners, each has also had its saints and advocates of righteousness. God's people are the salt of the earth and the light of the world. Without them, their witness, and their influence, the world would have come to an untimely end. We need but recall the age of Noah in which righteousness was limited to a single family. Unrighteousness was so prevalent that God sent the flood and started the race afresh after the destruction. Good men can and do influence society for the better. Human slavery, for instance, has been eliminated in virtually all the enlightened nations of the world. Temporal conditions in many areas of life have been markedly improved. Food, shelter, and clothing have become increasingly available to multiplied millions of people. In the United States even the poorest of its citizens are vastly better off than its poorest citizens were one hundred years ago.

The paradox of this age is that advanced technology, which has brought affluence and improved temporal conditions, has also brought new and graver problems threatening man's very existence. Science has extended man's life span, improved his health, increased his food supply, and heated and cooled his habitations; but it has also brought the atom bomb, poison gas, and germ warfare. Factories mass-produce cars, clothing, houses, and planes, but also pollute the atmosphere, poison the rivers, and make sewers out of the oceans. As one problem is solved, another develops. Because of sin and alienation from God, and despite the witness of the redeemed of God to his saving grace, man never quite makes it.

God's plan of the ages takes into account the fact that man cannot solve his problems on his own, nor will Satan help him, for Satan's chief purpose is to destroy man and defeat God. But God, through the God-man Jesus Christ, has a plan designed to do for man what he cannot do for himself. This plan is working out according to his purpose, to be fulfilled in his time and to accomplish what he wants done. Nations will rise to their summits only to sink into oblivion —but God's plan of the ages moves on—slowly, perhaps, but steadily. Satan's seemingly immovable and unconquerable forces will yield to divine invincibility until the world that was shall be again, until Paradise that was lost is regained, until God rules and reigns over all, until at the name of Jesus every knee shall bow and every tongue confess that he is the Christ, to the praise of the Father.

III. WHO THE DEVIL IS HE?

Satan, God's chief adversary, was created by God originally as an angel of light before the worlds came into being. He was the fairest of all creatures to whom the highest station was given and above whom no one stood except God himself. The tragedy was that this "sun of the morning," who shined brightly and rose higher than any other creature, fell farthest, and became the darkest blot on all of God's handiwork.

Although Scripture tells very little about how Satan fell, it does tell us a great deal about what he became when he fell, the corresponding results in the universe, and the works of this malign being today.

The Apostle John says that Satan sinned "from the beginning" (1 John 3:8). Evidently envying God, he sought to supplant him, revolted, and challenged God in all of his creation and plan, which he will continue to do until the end of time. Satan by his sin was transformed into a wicked being whom the Bible pictures as proud, saying that a bishop should not be a novice, "lest being lifted up with pride he fall into the condemnation of the devil" (1 Tim. 3:6).

The devil is also presumptuous. To be convinced, one

need only read the first chapter of the Book of Job as Satan presented himself before God to begin his campaign to ruin Job. He asked God, "Doth Job fear God for nought?" (1:9); later he said, "Skin for skin, yea all that a man hath will he give for his life" (2:4), intimating that Job remained true to God when his wealth and children were taken only because he still had his own life. He sneeringly suggested that if touched in his flesh, Job would curse God. Satan sought to make Jesus presume on his Father by daring him to cast himself down from the pinnacle of the temple, expecting the Father to send angels to protect Jesus in his presumption (Matt. 4:5, 6).

Satan is also very wicked, for John commends believers who have "overcome the wicked one" (1 John 2:13). He is subtle according to Genesis 3:1, shown in his subversion of Adam and Eve. Paul makes special mention of how Satan "beguiled Eve through his subtlety" (2 Cor. 11:3), warning believers that he still is subtle and works on God's children just as he worked on Eve.

The devil is a powerful being, described by Paul in Ephesians as "the prince of the power of the air" (2:2), as one of the "rulers of the darkness of this world" (6:12). Not only subtle and powerful, he is deceitful as well: "Satan himself is transformed into an angel of light" (2 Cor. 11:14). He pretends to be what he is not, presenting himself to men as a sheep while he is really a wolf garbed in sheep's clothing.

Satan shows no mercy or compassion. His unclean cohorts drove the man of Gadara mad, and an unclean spirit is described as having torn one child from within (Luke 9:39). Peter says, "the devil, as a roaring lion, walketh about, seeking whom he may devour" (1 Pet. 5:8). This is the character of the one with whom we battle, the person whose existence and personality some would deny.

God created Adam and Eve sinless. Satan, however, had

access to them and was the agent who brought about their fall. Some do not really believe the biblical account of the fall or that Adam and Eve were individuals known by those names; nor do they think that all members of the human race sprang from them. Naturalistic evolutionists, in particular, do not believe in original sin or the fall of man, but think man commenced his long journey in a primitive state and has been moving upward ever since. The biblical account is quite different, for it says Adam was the first man (1 Cor. 15:45) and pictures a paradise (Gen. 2:8) occupied by perfect beings who sinned and retrogressed, went backwards, not forwards. Scripture says Satan solicited Adam and Eve to sin, asserting also that all human beings have sprung from their union (see the genealogy of Luke 3:23-38). When they sinned, something happened to the world of nature and the world of men.

First of all, nature was corrupted and came under the dominion of Satan, to be taken from him only by force and against his will. God placed a curse on nature for man's sake (Gen. 3:17-19). A holy God could not permit sinful man to live in a perfect paradise which he would have spoiled in any event, as he spoils everything he touches. So God drove man out of the Garden of Eden into a cursed world. The ground was cursed to bring forth thorns and thistles. Man would eat the fruit of the earth which he would gain only by laborious and painful toil. A field does not bring forth good fruit of itself but brings forth weeds. When good seeds are planted, the earth has to be prepared, and the weeds have to be removed as the good plant begins to grow. Always man is against nature, fighting for survival in the face of the curse placed upon the earth by God because of sin. Satan loves watching man's agony as he battles nature; he rejoices that man has been cast so low and has lost his inheritance in Eden.

Secondly, man was lost and undone, suffering death as a

consequence of sin. Thus what happened to nature is nothing compared to what happened to man, who fell into the clutches of the devil. The picture of man's retrogression is painted by the Apostle Paul in Romans: when men knew God they did not glorify him as God but their foolish hearts were darkened. Turning away from the living God to idolatry, they dishonored their own bodies by perverting the natural relations between the sexes, and God gave them up. Paul describes them as "being filled with all unrighteousness, fornication, wickedness, covetousness, maliciousness; full of envy, murder, debate, deceit, malignity; whisperers, backbiters, haters of God, despiteful, proud, boasters, inventors of evil things, disobedient to parents, without understanding, covenant breakers, without natural affection, implacable, unmerciful: who knowing the judgment of God, that they which commit such things are worthy of death, not only do the same, but have pleasure in them that do them" (Rom. 1:29-32).

Men do not become sinners but are sinners; men do not become lost, but are already so; they do not come under bondage to Satan but are already under bondage to him by birth. As sons of the devil, all are on their way to destruction and do not need to be condemned, for they are condemned already (John 8:44; 3:18). This is what Satan has wrought for men and there is no escape, unless by the second birth they cease to be the sons of Satan and become children of God. Only those who come to God through Jesus Christ become new creatures, freed from their bondage, sorrow, and night. All others belong to Satan for time and eternity. His end is their end, his destiny their destiny.

Because men belong to Satan by birth and nature, he uses them for his purposes. One of the most tragic incidents in biblical history is that moment when Satan himself entered Judas Iscariot. "Then entered Satan into Judas surnamed

Iscariot" (Luke 22:3). To suppose that Satan uses only bad or what we might call really wicked men, such as Adolf Hitler, Joseph Stalin, or Benito Mussolini, is incorrect. To be sure, he used them and those like them, but he also uses men the world calls good, who may even be highly moral and whose lives seem as good as those of some who call themselves Christians. Indeed, "good men" may make better tools in the hands of Satan than bad ones.

Wherever there is mischief afoot, Satan is sure to be involved. He is the one who precipitates wars, encourages men in their lusts, causes men to question the Word of God, and tells men they can play with sin and win. He stands by every drunkard's side. He peers out of the window of every house of prostitution. He watches over the shoulder of every thief. He feeds words into the mouth of every blasphemer. He controls the mind and thoughts of every pornographer. He sits beside the statesmen in the chancellories of the world as they decide the destiny of nations. He attends all the meetings of the United Nations. He laughs silently beside the graves of his victims and claps his hands with glee when men slide into eternity without the knowledge of Jesus Christ.

The question can rightly be asked whether the devil is really at work in the world and what evidences we have for it. John states that "he who commits sin is of the devil; for the devil has sinned from the beginning. The reason the Son of God appeared was to destroy the works of the devil" (1 John 3:8). Thus in a general sense every work of sin has its ultimate root in Satan.

The devil uses the love of money to occasion much sin today, evidenced by the drug traffic which flourishes because of the fantastic profits that can be made from it, and pornography merchants who pander to debased appetites for financial gain.

The film industry increasingly caters to voyeurism and lasciviousness. Many argue that the worst films have redeeming social value, and even some clergymen openly support films that are prurient and spiritually deadening. In the United States the freedom of speech principle has been extended beyond anything allowed by the courts a hundred years ago or intended by the framers of the constitution. Whereas those who broke the law of God a hundred years ago acknowledged its existence, sinners today know no law.

The devil is busy with soothsayers, astrologists, palm readers, and fortune tellers. Seances are popular and even so noted a figure as the late Bishop James Pike was involved in contacting the spirit of his son, who had committed suicide in a New York hotel.

Satanology, with its numerous "churches," advocates demon worship and "Black masses." Christian psychologists and psychiatrists tell of cases of demon possession, and Christian churches are resuming the practice of exorcism.

Indeed, Satan, the prince of this world (John 12:31), has power, knows how to use it, and will stoop to making up his own rules for every occasion. Before any human being ever perverted Scripture, Satan was a past master of that game. This was his strategy in the temptation of Jesus (see Matt. 4:6). He quotes and misquotes Scripture, uses it in part when it suits him, and never hesitates to take it out of context. Jesus called Satan a liar and the father of lies (John 8:44).

Satan hinders the advance of the Gospel, for Paul says he has "blinded the minds of them which believe not, lest the light of the glorious gospel of Christ, who is the image of God, should shine unto them" (2 Cor. 4:4). One of the greatest of all Jesus' parables is that of the sower, which Jesus interpreted for the benefit of his disciples, carefully explaining to them that the seed is the Word of God. "When any one heareth the word of the kingdom," he said, "and understandeth it not, then cometh the wicked one (Satan), and catcheth away that which was sown in his heart. This is he which received seed by the way side" (Matt. 13:19). Satan will allow anything except the conversion of the sinner and will try to steal the seed of the Word from the soil of the heart so that it will not germinate eternal life. Satan always opposes the work of God. Zechariah wrote, "And he shewed me Joshua the high priest standing before the angel of the Lord, and Satan standing at his right hand to resist him" (3:1). The experience of the Apostle Paul was this: "Wherefore we would have come unto you, even I Paul, once and again; but Satan hindered us" (1 Thess. 2:18).

Satan has power to work lying wonders that can deceive even those numbered among the elect. In principle it is always true that the real can be counterfeited. There are counterfeit monies, counterfeit paintings, and counterfeit signatures, all which of necessity presuppose the real. False Christians and counterfeit speaking in tongues exist in the spiritual realm; Satan even performs counterfeit miracles, lying wonders intended to deceive men. Paul speaks about "him, whose coming is after the working of Satan with all power and signs and lying wonders" (2 Thess. 2:9). In the Revelation, St. John says, "I saw three unclean spirits . . . For they are the spirits of devils, working miracles, which go forth unto the kings of the earth and of the whole world, to gather them to the battle of that great day of God Almighty" (Rev. 16:13, 14).

Satan does not work alone (Matt. 25:41), for multitudes of fallen angels are his cohorts (see Mark 5:9). Jude speaks of angels "which kept not their first estate." The Scripture says elsewhere that angels are very numerous, very powerful, aware of what is happening throughout the world, and can go from place to place instantaneously. Satan himself is not actually omnipresent, but is virtually so by reason of the number of fallen angels at his command. The demons of Scripture are fallen angels who take up their abode in men for evil purposes, who have the same powers as the unfallen but use them for wickedness.

Satan is neither omnipotent nor free to do everything he pleases. Prince of this world he may be, but the Prince of Peace has come and dealt him a death blow (John 12:31). Although Satan's work is not yet finished and his doom still in the future, God has put a leash on him. He can go only so far and no further. There is the mystery of why God permits Satan to continue for as much as another hour, or why he fits into the cosmic plan of salvation. Nevertheless, God assures his people that he is for them and greater than the one who is against them, that Satan's doom is sure, that he is to be resisted by the people of God (Matt. 4:11), and that for them there is victory over the wicked one.

What is important for the Christian to understand is that he lives in an evil and dying world, that Satan is not only the prince of the power of the air but also the prince of this world; to be at home in it is to be at home with Satan. The Christian is to be crucified to the world, for his true citizenship is in heaven. The friend of the world is no friend of God, therefore the Christian must always be on his guard. There is no moment when he can safely let down the bars because this is a warfare, a life of struggle in which nothing delights Satan more than to see a Christian become a backslider. All hell rejoices in the fall of a single saint, even as all heaven rejoices in the salvation of a single sinner.

The great question every man must ask himself is, "Whose servant am I—the servant of Satan or the servant of the Lord Jesus Christ?" How a man answers determines his destiny, not only in this world temporarily controlled by

Satan, but also in the world to come, which will be controlled by God and closed to all defilement. For that is one of righteousness, truth, justice, love, and purity, a world without sin or Satan, ruled over by the Lamb slain from the foundation of the world.

IV. CHOOSING A LIFE STYLE

When a man becomes a Christian he is not removed from the world. His translation takes place either at death or, if he should then happen to be alive, at the coming of the Lord Jesus. But until he dies or Jesus comes, he is very much in the world. His heart and his head may be in heaven, but his feet are on the earth where he has to live day by day.

The Christian is a pilgrim, but should never forget that while his true citizenship is in heaven, he still retains a citizenship on earth (1 Pet. 2:11; Phil. 3:20). As a member of two kingdoms, the kingdom of God and the kingdom of Caesar, he is called to live by the principles of God's kingdom while existing physically for a time in the kingdom of Caesar (John 14:15). This unusual kind of life is not as bad as it first appears, for there are laws of life that are common to both kingdoms. Problems generally arise because some men deny the existence of God's laws of life or, if they acknowledge them, refuse to abide by them. Even Christians can thwart God's laws when they, like men of the world, fail to obey them.

The Christian, however, is different from the non-Christian in that he has experienced a second or a new birth

(1 Pet. 1:23) and has been redeemed by the Holy Spirit. Subsequent to regeneration the believer starts his new life. He is not yet perfect and will not be glorified (i.e., made perfectly like the Lord Jesus) until the end of the age. Meanwhile he enters into that period of his new life, between justification and glorification, which we call sanctification. To be sanctified means to be holy. Salvation is both a final or completed act and a process. Thus the Christian is already positionally sanctified, indeed glorified (Rom. 8:30), but that which is his in principle must be worked out in practice daily (Phil. 2:12). This is the process part of salvation.

The Christian is different not only because he has experienced the new birth, but also because he experiences a new estrangement. Before becoming a Christian he was the enemy of God; he loved the world and the world loved him. But once reconciled to God he becomes estranged from the world. Formerly the world loved him, whereas now it hates him (John 15:18). So man, whether saved or lost, experiences alienation in this life either from God or from the world. Jesus said that every disciple is "not of the world" (John 15:19), but he also said that the Christian is *in* the world. Had he been removed at salvation there would be no further estrangement. But it doesn't happen this way. Jesus said that as the Father sent him into the world, so he has sent his disciples into the world (John 17:18). This is the great paradox of the Christian life: we live in the world but are not of the world.

Jesus told his disciples a great truth, often overlooked or misunderstood even by students of the Bible, that in the world the Christian will have tribulation (John 16:33). Some make the mistake of supposing that if one really lives the Christian life then tribulation will not be his lot. Quite the contrary. He will have tribulation because he tries to live the Christian life, and not infrequently, the closer he comes to living the good life, the more apt he is to experience greater tribulation. No Christian should rejoice over the absence of tribulation but rather should be deeply concerned when it is not present. Its absence may well mean that the quality of his Christian life is defective.

Tribulation proceeds from Satan, the archenemy of God and of God's people. God does not experience tribulation, being beyond the reach of Satan. Therefore Satan must attack God by attacking God's people. When he cuts them down and wins victories over them he has successfully struck a blow against God himself. He can say to God: "This is your servant whom you have redeemed. Look at him! He serves me and my plan of the ages better than he serves you and your plan of the ages." This ought not to be, but too often is, in the life of believers.

Satan is powerfully determined to undermine and defeat the children of God. Skillful and diabolical, he has an infinite variety of means at his disposal to accomplish his evil designs (Job 2:4; 2 Cor. 11:14; Eph. 6:11). Rarely attacking the Christian frontally or bombarding him with gross power, he uses subtlety and practices gradualism instead (Gen. 3:1; 2 Cor. 11:3). It is said that if a frog is dumped into a pail of hot water it will leap out immediately, but if placed in cold water that is heated gradually it will remain and be boiled to death.

The Christian life is a continual spiritual warfare, part of God's plan of the ages which does not end until death (1 Tim 6:12). There is every reason to approach it with fear and trembling, but there is no reason to run away from it. Perhaps the worst counsel anyone can give a new convert is to tell him, "Become a Christian and all your problems will be solved." This is a great distortion and incredibly poor advice. "Become a Christian and your troubles really begin" is closer to the truth, so long as one does not stop there. God uses tribulation from Satan to purify the Christian, strengthen him, and make him more and more like Jesus Christ. In the midst of tribulation God makes visible his delivering power and brings the believer to a place of fuller and deeper trust in him.

If the Christian thinks he can escape or lessen the intensity of tribulation by fleeing from the world, he is unrealistic. The monastics in earlier ages sought to do this, but found out that hairshirts, flagellation, and renunciation neither kept the world from them nor sheltered them from the darts of the wicked one. Man's problems are located in his heart as well as his environment. Changing the environment may indeed alter externals, even lessen temptation, but this will not change the heart. However, if the heart is changed then the power of the environment makes much less difference. Jesus Christ could live fully and sinlessly in the world, uncontaminated by its allures, because his heart was right.

THE MISSION OF THE BELIEVER

If the lot of the Christian is to endure tribulation in the world, what then is his role? What is he called to do and to be? The mission of the believer in this present evil age is twofold: to witness to the grace of God in Jesus and to be as salt of the earth, making the presence and the power of God known among men. This mission involves both proclamation and service. The Church is in the world to bear witness against the world and to announce its approaching doom, while at the same time calling men to repent of their sins and have faith in Jesus Christ for salvation. Each Christian, as a member of Christ's body, has a similar function. Because he cannot exercise this ministry if he removes himself from the world, he therefore accepts the divine call to live in the world on its behalf and for the sake of Jesus Christ. But his ministry or mission is not fulfilled in proclamation alone.

In addition to proclaiming the Gospel the Christian is

called to a life of service to Jesus Christ, to his fellow believers, and to the world (2 Cor. 4:5). Like salt and leaven he is to influence and affect all levels of society in his secular as well as religious pursuits. Whether a bus driver, the president of a large corporation, or a politician, the Christian is called to serve the world as a member of God's kingdom, and therefore in a real sense is never engaged in a secular pursuit. In a place or a position regarded as secular he is called to fulfill his vocation as a Christian and is not, or at least never should be, simply a bus driver, corporation president or politician, but a Christian bus driver, corporation president, or politician, and this should motivate him to be the best he can in his field.

The Christian who is summoned by God to a so-called secular pursuit is commanded, in that pursuit, to live according to the principles of the kingdom of God. "Impossible!" someone will say. Not so at all. Difficult, yes, but impossible, no. There is one qualification that must be added, however. Some occupations in themselves are fundamentally incompatible with the Christian vocation. It is inconceivable that God would call a woman to a life of prostitution so that she could witness to Christ's saving power to her clients. God does not call his saints to lives of criminality, thievery, fraud, and chicanery, but to pursuits that are good or neutral, which can be used righteously or wickedly depending on how the person decides to conduct himself in his particular calling.

In any event, the call of God does mean that the Christian is to work for justice, manifest love to all men, and endeavor as far as possible to make the principles of the kingdom of God regnant and operative among men. He will never wholly succeed, since the kingdom in its fulness cannot come until the King himself returns; often his best efforts will yield no discernible fruit. Nevertheless, he is called to a life of faithfulness, not necessarily to a life of success. For

it is faithfulness on which the judgment of God is based
(1 Cor. 4:2).

CHANGING SOCIETY

One question which cannot be avoided concerns to what
extent the Christian should work for laws that will bind unbelievers, laws that are in keeping with the teachings of the
Bible but to which unbelievers take exception. The issue
here is not the mission of the Church as Church but of the
individual Christian in Caesar's kingdom. Should he support,
if they already exist, or should he seek to have passed, laws
that forbid adultery, homosexuality, pornography, obscenity,
and other such activities? Or should he regard them as
private matters and conclude that unbelievers should be free
to live as they choose, according to their personal convictions and the light they have? This is a difficult question about
which there are differences of opinion.

We ought not obscure the fact that the existence of cultural patterns so different from biblical standards has caused
some groups of people to withdraw from the world and create small closed communities of their own. Failure to do
so, they felt, would lead inevitably to contamination which
would destroy their way of life and faith. Aware of kingdom
principles, desirous of glorifying God, because they were not
of the world, and fearful that being in the world would
result in conformity to it, they chose what they thought the
lesser of two evils. But this course is contrary to Christ's own
command: "I do not pray that thou shouldst take them out
of the world . . . So have I also sent them into the world"
(John 17:15, 18).

Since the Christian is called to witness in and to the world,
exposed to its evils, it is in his interest and the interest of
society for him to work for laws that are in accord with

biblical principles. Society is bound to be governed by laws representing one life view or another, and the Christian should endeavor, as far as possible, to embody his in legislative acts to improve society. Indeed, every Christian is called upon to use his influence to mold and remake society in accord with the laws of God, and he is negligent in his duty who refuses to do so.

There is ample evidence showing how civilizations have crumbled when vice and license prevailed. Laws were not made for righteous people but for malefactors and dissidents whose conduct is hurtful to society. The closer nations come to a system of law based on biblical standards, benefitting the world through the common grace of God, the less likely they are to disintegrate. The believer works to implement Christian principles in the structures of society because he is in the business of rescuing men from secular as well as spiritual destruction. It is also to his advantage and that of his children to live in a world and culture which have been Christianized as much as possible.

Satan is intensely interested in defeating efforts to make Christian principles normative in any culture. The evil influences of non-Christian cultures and standards are important to Satan only insofar as they aid in the ultimate destruction of men's souls. When wickedness abounds and God of necessity must step in to judge as he did in Noah's day and the time of Sodom and Gomorrah, Satan then knows the success of helping to denizen hell. The believer must seek to introduce some semblance of Christian standards to non-Christian cultures, for this constitutes a defeat for Satan and makes his work of subversion that much more difficult.

The believer has a role to play in the world in relation to his destiny. Knowing that the world is temporal (2 Cor. 4:18), he looks for that other city which has enduring foundations and whose builder and maker is God. The fashion of this world is passing away (1 Cor. 7:31); even while the Christian lives on earth he looks forward to eternity, his hope built on the assurance that he will be an inhabitant of the New Jerusalem that will come down from God out of heaven (Rev. 21:10). Yet while he is certain about his final destiny based on his faith in Jesus Christ, through whom he has been reconciled to God and made righteous, he has no particular assurance about the extent of the reward that will be given him in the new city of God. This is determined at the judgment seat of Christ, based upon his works, the quality of his life and the degree to which he has been faithful in his stewardship of the talents God has given him (2 Cor. 5:10).

Every believer will be called upon to give an account of his stewardship—for himself only and for no other (Rom. 14:10). This account will include both his good and bad deeds (2 Cor. 5:10). Scripture informs him that his works will be tested by fire to see whether they are perishable or permanent (1 Cor. 3:11 ff.). If consisting of wood, hay, and stubble, they will be consumed and he will enter glory saved but empty-handed, at best an unpleasant thought and something that should cause each to examine the quality of his life, and, where necessary, to mend his ways. In view of this, every Christian living in the world as he has been commanded must inquire as to what extent and degree he is *of* the world, remembering that: He who sows a thought reaps an act; he who sows an act reaps a habit; he who sows a habit reaps a life; he who sows a life reaps a destiny (Gal. 6:7). Having looked at the mission and destiny of the Christian it is time to examine the most important consideration of all—the life of the believer *in* the world.

THE BELIEVER IN THE WORLD

One way the Bible uses the word *world* (*kosmos* and *aion*) is quite derogatory, denoting a kind of person and style of life contrary to what God intended. Thus individual acts can never be isolated from the total life style of the Christian, because what one is and what one does are inextricably related. The perfect man lives the perfectly coordinated life; what he is and what he does are consistent with one another. He does not claim to be what his actions would deny. To the contrary, his actions reflect his profession and do not invalidate it.

The Scriptures refer to the kind of life that displeases God as worldly. Paul urged believers not to be pressed into the mold of the world, plainly suggesting that the Christian who is shaped after the fashion of the world has missed the target (Rom. 12:1,2). Obviously the world is spoken of in undesirable terms. But Paul, who warns against conformity to the world, does not here spell out precisely what he means by the term. One can infer that the world is something opposed to what God is and stands for, in which case the problem can be approached in one of two ways: either by finding what characteristics are common to the world and avoiding them or what characteristics are common to God and imitating them. In other words, if the world is characterized by lying, shun it; if God is characterized by truthfulness, imitate it.

Paul adds to our dilemma of defining the world when he speaks about Demas, who, he says, has "forsaken me, having loved this present world (*aion,* age)." Does he mean here the world that is, in contrast with a future world? Or does he mean a life style based upon Satan's pattern, against one introduced by Jesus Christ?

Paul says that the world is condemned, claiming that the

44

Christian who cares for the things of the world suffers defeat, and that the believer should be crucified to the world and the world crucified to him (1 Cor. 11:32; 7:33; Gal. 6:14). He condemns any life style that is "according to the course of this world" (Eph. 2:2), going so far as to say that the very "wisdom of the world is foolishness" (1 Cor. 3:19).

Jesus himself contrasted the present world with the new one, which will come fully and finally at the end of the age, and which he speaks of as present in a hidden fashion in this now existing evil world. He asks: "What shall it profit a man, if he shall gain the whole world (*kosmos*), and lose his own soul?" (Mk. 8:36). He speaks too of the "cares of this world" (*aion,* this age; Matt. 13:22; Mark 4:19), announces that this present world has already been judged (John 12:31), and refuses to pray for it (John 17:9). He says neither he nor his people are *of* this world although they are *in* it (John 15:18 ff.). This world of which Jesus speaks, its people, its works, and its life style, is condemned. Yet he wants this world to hear of him, to know that he has been sent to it, and yearns for it to believe on him (John 17:18 ff.). He identifies Satan as the prince of this world (John 16:11; 14:30) and claims that his (Christ's) kingdom is not of this world.

This world is part of Satan's dominion which is in conflict with Christ's kingdom. The Christian becomes a part of Christ's kingdom when he experiences the new birth, but continues to live in the world (i.e., in Satan's kingdom). He is called upon, however, to refuse voluntarily to identify with the world, instead to live up to the principles of the kingdom of God. In a world that rejects not only these principles but also their source, a fierce war is being waged against those who own allegiance to Christ.

This supplies a clue to the meaning of the world: whatever Satan is the world is; whatever Christ is the world is not. They are fundamentally different, like oil and water, so that no union between them is possible. Unlike the dialectic of Hegel and Marx, which posits a thesis and an antithesis joined to produce a new synthesis, Satan's kingdom and God's kingdom are antithetical but no synthesis is possible. Some Christians err in thinking it possible to have the best of two worlds, Satan's and God's. To follow this path is to lose God's world, and the traffic is all on a one way street—the wrong way.

The Apostle John articulates this cleavage between the kingdom of Satan and the kingdom of God: "Love not the world, neither the things that are in the world. If any man love the world, the love of the Father is not in him. For all that is in the world, the lust of the flesh, and the lust of the eyes, and the pride of life, is not of the Father, but is of the world. And the world passeth away, and the lust thereof: but he that doeth the will of God abideth for ever" (1 John 2:15-17).

Peter speaks of the corruption that is in the world and the pollutions of the world (2 Pet. 2:4; 2 Pet. 2:20). James says Christians are to keep themselves "unspotted from the world" (1:27), for the "friend of the world is the enemy of God" (4:4).

The world is clearly evil and opposed to God. The apostles took the world seriously, realized its dangers, and everywhere warned Christians to seek victory over it (1 John 5:4).

Any discussion of worldliness cannot avoid materialism, which has philosophical as well as existential implications. Materialism is by no means confined to those who have much of this world's goods. It is endemic among those having little of material things but wanting more.

Perhaps the chief contributor to the materialism of our day is the philosophy of Marxism. Central to its standpoint is the view that economic matters are determinative. Wholly devoid of anything spiritual, it concentrates solely on material things. Since the world is largely populated by the Have-nots, whose number is growing annually, Marxism has tremendous popular appeal. In effect it argues that the Haves are the oppressors of the Have-nots, locating the evil in the Mosaic command, "Thou shalt not steal," which is considered an economic device to perpetuate the ruling class and to keep the bulk of the people downtrodden. The wealthy are the bourgeoisie, the poor the proletariat. As these two classes are enemies, the proletariat is encouraged to eliminate the bourgeoisie by revolution, take over their wealth, and create a classless society where the prevailing principle will be "from each according to his ability, to each according to his need."

The emphasis of Marxism is on the material. Since the vast proportion of the world's people are poor, Marxism offers them the hope of more of the world's goods. To the poverty-stricken the appeal is tremendous. What have they got to lose? Their economic situation seemingly can get no worse. Any change is bound to be an improvement. To the hungry, possessionless masses, materialism is attractive. The fact that it offers no spiritual benefits seems unimportant when physical life itself is at stake.

It is not difficult to understand why men without Christianity would be attracted to Marxism with its materialistic framework, nor why those who do not believe in God or immortality concentrate their time and efforts on the material.

But materialism is a problem for Christians as well, one which may be a major temptation for them and to which they succumb all too easily. No one should dismiss the possible influence of Marxist thinking on Christians, who may deny Marxism in principle, but still fall prey to the materialism of that particular world view.

It should not be thought, however, that Marxism has introduced materialism into history, for materialism has always existed to challenge Christianity. Centuries before Karl Marx men were capitulating to materialism. Judas Iscariot sold Jesus for a few pieces of silver; King Solomon's heart was turned away from God by great riches and the presence of a thousand wives and concubines; King Ahab was a materialist who coveted Naboth's vineyard, despite the fact that he already had much more than he needed of this world's goods.

Jesus gave us the parable of the rich fool (Luke 12:13-21). A thoroughgoing materialist, he had enough but was not satisfied. Jesus said, "a man's life does not consist in the abundance of his possessions" (Luke 12:15). The rich fool thought it did and laid up treasure for himself on earth, all of which he left at death, only to discover that he was "not rich toward God."

In a very practical way materialism is a temptation to Christians today, working both on those who have little and on those who have much. The person with little wants more: a bigger house, a second home in the mountains or at the seashore, more cars, better clothing, fancier trips, more expensive restaurants, and a continually rising standard of living.

Materialism grows insidiously in the Christian heart and its true nature is often disguised: the thought life adjusts itself to material standards far beyond reasonable needs and makes these standards normative. Once regarded as normative they are accepted as biblical and justified as being in accord with the will of God. Not infrequently the acquisition of material things is regarded as God's special blessing for being "good," and Christians tend to regard themselves as recipients of these things by reason of merit due to their hard work. The fact that millions of true believers languish in poverty is overlooked or explained away by thinking these people lazy or unproductive.

In the United States, perhaps the richest of all nations, more Christians have capitulated to materialistic lives than anywhere else. In the final analysis it is no more than putting *things* before God, of seeking first the kingdom of man rather than the kingdom of God. It is easy to forget the biblical principle that the things that are seen are temporal, while the things that are not seen are eternal.

To suppose that materialism is limited to the possessions of money, lands, houses, and furniture would be imprudent. The materialist may also seek for himself the more intangible trappings of power, fame, and applause, although these are rarely attained without money and other material things. But they are an expression of materialism and represent a commitment to priorities other than God.

We cannot suppose the man who does have much of this world's goods is automatically a materialist. Abraham had wealth but his affection was set on the things of God. He "looked forward to the city which has foundations, whose builder and maker is God" (Heb. 11:10). It was said of Moses, "He considered abuse suffered for the Christ greater wealth than the treasures of Egypt, for he looked to the reward . . . he endured as seeing him who is invisible" (Heb. 11:26, 27).

Not infrequently materialism is the disease of older people who seek a sense of security in bank accounts and houses, who substitute present riches for trust in God even while piously mouthing phrases about their faith. Trusting God is easier when you have a million dollars than when you have nothing.

In the Sermon on the Mount Jesus clearly distinguishes

between God and materialism: "You cannot serve God and mammon" (Matt. 6:24). But he enlarges on this by commanding his people not to be "anxious about your life, what you shall eat or what you shall drink, nor about your body, what you shall put on." The birds are fed and the lilies clothed by God. The Gentiles are materialists, for their concern is what they eat and wear. But God takes care of his people if they put first things first. "Seek first his kingdom and his righteousness, and all these things shall be yours as well" (Matt. 6:25 ff.).

The Christian materialist finds it easy to conform his actions to his materialistic viewpoint. The Christian mechanic who follows his boss's order to charge for work he did not perform and parts he did not install in order to keep his job is a case in point. The accountant who keeps false books to cover shady dealings or defraud the government on income taxes is a similar illustration.

For years to come Americans will be faced with the Watergate scandal. Here, people who professed a commitment to law and order and the Judeo-Christian moral ideals broke laws out of loyalty to their leaders and in order to maintain their positions in the ruling structures. Phones were tapped, offices were broken into, large sums of money were mishandled, lies were told, and cover-up activities became commonplace. The materialist is at home in this environment which makes a clear commitment to temporal things. This leads inevitably to a consideration of transcending importance:

CHOOSING ONE'S LIFE STYLE

Before discussing particular personal conduct in the bruising battle against the world, one vital matter should be faced having to do with the problem of commitment and choice of a life style. The question is unimportant so long as the believer has not expressed a desire for, or displayed any firm resolve to seek, victory over the world. If his heart attachment is not centered on Jesus Christ and he has not made up his mind to pursue holiness, without which no man shall see the Lord (Heb. 12:14), he is lopsided, defective, and defeated.

There is little need for the Christian to wrestle with the implications involved in the struggle against the world if he does not intend to struggle. To listen politely, nod the head in agreement, and pay lip service to a principle one does not wish to follow is dishonest and hypocritical. Young people today are angry with their elders who profess allegiance to one set of principles but practice something quite different. Not that young people outperform their elders. Indeed, they do no better except in the areas they choose to magnify, and then pride themselves falsely on being better because their practice conforms to their arbitrary standards. The equation works out something like this: (1) the elders support higher standards but do not keep them; therefore they are hypocrites; (2) the youth on the other hand keep their own lower standards; therefore they are "honest" and have integrity. The elders fail because they do not live up to their own professed standards, while the younger ones fail for a different reason: they practice what they believe, but if their beliefs are inconsistent with the moral law, they end up in the same condemnation with their elders.

In talking about the Christian's life style in relation to particular acts one thing must be made clear: he must choose his life style first, then conform his acts to that choice, not vice versa. The reason for this is plain. If my acts precede my choice, then the life style is determined by the deeds; but if the life style is supposed to determine what deeds I should and should not do, my actions in any particular situation must follow, not precede, the commitment. It is true, of course, that I may fail at points in being faithful to my commitment; to do so is to act inconsistently. But if I act before I have chosen a life style, I have no grounds for making any decision except whim and caprice, which are not adequate guides for living the good life.

The issue for the Christian is limited to two options: God or the devil. There is no third possibility. Nor can these two basic options be synthesized. Both are adversaries with their own kingdoms. This means that if I am committed to one option, but practice what belongs to the other, I am deceiving myself about my basic commitment. In that event integrity demands that I acknowledge my real commitment to the other option, or bring my acts into line with the one I have professed but not practiced. The choice the Christian makes for God has a negative as well as positive aspect. Negatively he must say: "I renounce the works of the devil." Positively he must say: "I cling to God and to the principles of his kingdom."

In talking about the Christian and his choice of a life in conformity to the world or conformity to God, must we not ask whether it is possible for anyone to choose deliberately to be conformed to the world and be a Christian, or if he is a Christian, to remain in a state of grace? It is difficult to imagine that anyone who has been born again and justified could or would opt *in principle* for conformity to the world. Anyone who does leaves open the question whether he has ever really experienced the grace of God. This person must ask himself seriously whether he is a Christian at all.

We know that justification is different from glorification, that between the time one is justified and glorified he must go through the process of sanctification. During this period, which lasts until death, the believer will not be sinlessly perfect. But if he is a true Christian he will intend to make holiness, not worldliness, the principle of his life. This we assume is the intention of those who read this book. For them the question now is, "What *is* worldliness and what decisions in life are permissible or illicit, either by clear statement from Scripture or by inference from principles laid down in Scripture?"

WORLDLINESS DEFINED

The dictionary defines being worldly as: "relating to the concerns of this life as distinguished from those of the life to come." The trouble with this definition is that it does not seem to do justice to the biblical data, suggesting that anyone who takes thought for the things of this life is worldly. Not so at all. Paul says that, "If anyone does not provide for his relatives, and especially for his own family, he has disowned the faith and is worse than an unbeliever" (1 Tim. 5:8). Moreover, Paul discovered that some Thessalonians had stopped working for spiritual reasons, believing that Christ had come or was coming immediately. Paul rebuked them saying, "keep away from any brother who is living in idleness . . . we were not idle when we were with you, we did not eat anyone's bread without paying . . . If anyone will not work, let him not eat" (2 Thess. 3:6 ff.).

Surely being spiritual does not mean being blithely oblivious to those things that are part of our humanity and physical life. But it does mean that the Christian is to be consistent in giving first place to the world that is to come. The spiritual aspect of life should control and dominate the physical and material aspects. Worldliness, then, is generally an attitude or a frame of mind that leaves out the spiritual dimension and concentrates beyond the proper boundaries on temporal things. Indeed, it is anything that is contrary to the expressed will of God or which runs counter to the mind of Christ.

The wrong word, the curse word, the lascivious glance, gluttony, immodest dress, excess of drink, even failure to get adequate sleep, are evidences of worldliness. The world-ling is headed in the wrong direction; the Spirit-filled Christian is headed in the right direction, even though his journey may be slow, or momentarily halted. The direction, not the speed of the journey, is basic. When one is moving away from the ideal, speed may hasten the journey, but moving slowly and casually is ultimately just as bad. How one travels —by plane, by auto or on foot—is not the decisive issue. The direction is what counts.

The Apostle John stated decisively that worldliness comprises the lust of the flesh, the lust of the eyes, and the pride of life (1 John 2:16), having to do with the sins of the spirit, the sins of the thought life, and the sins of the physical body. Few sins fall outside these three categories; some fall into one category alone, others embrace two or all three. If particular things can be identified as the lust of the flesh, the lust of the eyes, or the pride of life, they are to be shunned. Anything that does not fall in these categories may be done. This means that there are some prohibitions in life, a thought that is resisted increasingly by many who argue that either this will restrict their freedom or that nothing is intrinsically wrong.

Here the Christian faces an age-old dilemma, something that the modern mind likes to suppose it has discovered for the first time. It is basically a struggle over legalism versus license, over law versus grace, over absolutes versus relatives. This problem is compounded by the prevalent sociological idea that all moral standards are in effect taboos that have their beginnings in particular cultural situations, so that what may be wrong at one time in one culture may be right in another setting and at a different time. Since all cultures are relative, all actions are relative as well. There is a limited or partial truth in this, of course.

The Christian believes in divine revelation, holding that

God has declared some things always to be wrong. But people and cultures, even those that are professedly Christian, either tend to add to the list of what God has prohibited (legalism) or to slice away from and relativize it (antinomianism). This is what situation ethics does today.

Perhaps the best known exponent of this creed is Joseph Fletcher, an Episcopal theological seminary professor who openly declares, "I am prepared to argue that Christian obligation calls for lies and adultery and fornication and theft and promise-breaking and killing, sometimes, depending on the situation." He is saying that there are no absolutes. The Christian may be called upon to commit any of the sins prohibited in the Ten Commandments; only the individual himself can make the decision, and that can be determined only in the situation itself. No one outside the situation, including God, can tell him what to do; nor can anyone pass judgment on him as to the rightness or wrongness of his decision. He is judge and jury, lawgiver and subject at the same time. He is a law to himself. This philosophy of conduct effectively negates the law of God, even as it appeals to an undefined and fuzzy "law of love" that is supposed to come from the very Scriptures it repudiates. Logic and consistency, in this view, are the characteristics of small minds. So out goes consistency.

We have stated that the Christian is in the world even though he is not of the world. He must face the devil and all his works and temptations. He has a role and a mission to fulfill, the success of which depends on his choice of a life style. If he chooses the life that pleases the devil he will be a worldly Christian; if he chooses that which pleases God he will be a spiritual one. But when he has deliberately chosen a truly Christian life style, he is not then delivered from problems, for he is still faced with the temptations of the world, the flesh and the devil. But he knows that God has laid down some absolutes which have to do with his personal conduct, some things he is commanded to do and some things he is commanded to shun. So now we turn our attention to these laws of God.

V. ACCENTING THE POSITIVE

In the last chapter we said that everybody, in one fashion or another, selects a life-style for himself. The life-style we have proposed is the Christian one. But that which is accepted in principle must be worked out in everyday living. This means that there are some things the Christian will do and others that he will shun.

It is easy to lay down a whole list of "don'ts," and there are, in fact, don'ts in the Christian life. But these should be preceded by the positives. If there are actions to be avoided, there are others to be cultivated and sought after. In general, the Decalogue (or the moral law of Moses) comprises the essential commandments of God for his people in all ages. The Ten Commandments (Exodus 20) are generally divided into two tables. The first table of the law has a heavy accent on the positive; it tells us a great deal about some things we are to do. It is well, therefore, to begin our discussion by speaking first of those things we ought to do.

There is a sense in which any positive command can be asserted negatively and negative commands asserted positively. This is easy to illustrate. In the second table of the law we are told, "Thou shalt not bear false witness." This could be made positive by rewording it, "Thou shalt always tell the truth." The first table of the law says, "Remember the sabbath day to keep it holy." It could be restated, "Do not make the sabbath day unholy." Jesus made two positive assertions out of both tables of the law: "Thou shalt love the Lord thy God . . . and thy neighbor as thyself," (Mark 12:30, 31). Let us first take a quick look at the affirmative aspect of the law of God.

Everywhere in Scripture we are told to love God and put him first. There is only one true God, which is why the Ten Commandments begin with the positive assertion, "I am the Lord your God" (Ex. 20:1). All that follows is based upon the presupposition contained in this declaration. All other gods are false, and indeed have no real being. In this sense the first commandment opposes polytheism, but its accent is positive. There is but one God and he is the God and Father of our Lord Jesus Christ, the God of the Christian Scriptures. All men are called to love him, and loving him means giving him first place in their hearts and in their lives. Nothing can be allowed to come between them and the Lord God. This was precisely the recurring sin of the Israelites. Again and again they forgot God and put something before him. This can be illustrated in a number of ways from the Old Testament.

Of Uzziah it was said that "as long as he sought the Lord, God made him prosper" (2 Chron. 26:5). But when God prospered him and made him strong we are told that "he grew proud, to his destruction. For he was false to the Lord as his God, and entered the temple of the Lord to burn incense on the altar of incense" (v. 16). When he did this, God caused leprosy to break out on his forehead at the same time Uzziah was offering the incense. Had Uzziah truly loved God, he would have had respect for the law of God which assigned the Levites the task of burning incense. To begin with, he was not a Levite, nor was he a priest of God. Even the king, who was sovereign, could not do everything he pleased. He was neither less bound, nor more bound, to God and his commandments than the humblest Israelite. But there was a significant difference between the humbler people and the king. To him much had been given; from him much was required. Thus the same act performed by an ordinary Israelite would equally have placed that person in wrong relationship to God and brought divine judgment. But the king represented in a peculiar sense both God and the people. For Uzziah, as king, to do what he did, introduced a more heinous note and his sin was far more reprehensible.

2 Chronicles 20:33 states, "The people had not yet set their hearts upon the God of their fathers." Uzziah, whom we have just mentioned, represents one individual in whom we see the corporate sin of the people laid bare. We cannot and should not read into this the idea that none of them were faithful. Plainly, however, the hearts of the people on the whole were far from God. Years before, Elijah faced a similar situation (1 Kings, 18:20 ff.). Not only were the people guilty of failing to set their hearts on the God of their fathers, but they went far beyond this to bow down and worship another god, Baal. The situation was so grave that only 7,000 people had not bowed their knees to Baal. Elijah asked the question on Mount Carmel, "Who is the true God?" Thereafter he proved that Jehovah was God, and challenged the people to make a genuine choice—either Jehovah or Baal.

The God who demands the allegiance of his people is purposeful, sovereign, loving, and redemptive. He wants the voluntary, but undivided, affection of those who profess him. In his love he wants to bless his people and give them all they need in this life and in the life to come. He says to his people, "Love me and live." It needs to be said that men often revolt, as much against the idea of what they are to do positively, as against what they are forbidden to do. To tell men they must love God, a positive command, is just as onerous and objectionable to them as to tell them they should *not* commit adultery, covet, steal, or lie. It sounds so much more convincing to argue in opposition to a negative Christianity, but any objection leveled against the "thou shalt nots" must be seen for what it really is: a denial of the affirmative command of the first table of the law as expressed in the words of Jesus, "Thou shalt love the Lord thy God with all thine heart, and with all thy soul, and with all thy mind . . . " (Mk. 12:30).

Now if God is really God, men owe him more than love. Love must be transformed into affirmative action. He has commanded those who profess to love him to gather together for common worship of him. There is therefore no place for a solitary Christianity. As soon as a man is rightly related to God, he becomes a member of the body of Christ which has other members all belonging to one another. It is true, of course, that a man alone can worship God. But it is also true that God has commanded corporate worship, for believers are not to neglect the assembling of themselves together (Heb. 10:25). God has brought the Church into being and demands that his people be related to his body through the Church. He has also given elders and deacons for the supervision and oversight of the Church, and ordained that the Word of God should be preached in it.

No one can object to home Bible classes and to informal gatherings of believers, or to interest and participation in para-ecclesial organizations. But if these become substitutes for the ordered ministry of the Church, with the sacraments or ordinances of baptism and the Lord's Supper overlooked or forgotten, then those who follow this pattern are not loving

God as they ought, for love must act obediently to the positive commands of God.

Nowhere does the Bible overlook the fact that people who do not worship the true God often worship false ones. The Bible declares that there is only one true God and that all other gods are false. The great sin against the true God is to pay allegiance to other gods, which is precisely what the Israelites did repeatedly. Aaron made a golden calf at the behest of the people, while Moses was alone with God on Mount Sinai (Ex. 32:1 ff.). The people later turned to the worship of Baal at the forbidden "high places," and frequently turned to the gods of the nations around them. They forsook God, who had delivered them from Egypt and brought them into the land of promise. Their apostasy not infrequently included the worship of images. We should remember how Jacob's wife Rachel stole her father Laban's household gods. When he located Jacob and his hosts, she hid them beneath a saddle which she sat upon, pretending she would not rise for her father because she was pregnant (Gen. 31:33 ff.).

He who loves God knows that God is a spirit and cannot be represented by wood or stone (John 4:24). Therefore, the one who loves God will make no graven images nor bow down before any representation of God. The history of religion is the history of men bowing down before images of wood and stone and investing them with a false reality. In our day, there is less of this sort of thing among Western nations and educated people, although lands like India and Japan are still filled with idols. Many people think themselves too wise to be fooled by graven images, but they break this demand of God for singleminded devotion in other ways: fame, fortune, and power often become substitute gods in the heart, even when no visible image is constructed.

Even worse in this age is widespread atheism. But even

atheists turn toward some kind of god. In place of the true God man is often enthroned and humanism becomes their religion. Such deification of man is idolatry. To try to determine whether humanism is better or worse than polytheism is useless; for whatever man worships other than the true God separates him from God and salvation, and to speak about being closer to, or farther from God, makes little difference in this instance.

We should observe that non-Christian religions, while they are false and their adherents lost outside of Christ, still have some serviceable features that belong to the realm of God's common grace. Most religions bear witness to some of the elements contained in God's earliest self-revelation to man. The Confucian maxim, the Silver Rule, "Thou shalt not do unto others what you would not have others do unto you," is a true reflection of the Golden Rule of Jesus and witnesses to a universal truth. Confucianism is not adequate in a soteriological sense, for men cannot be saved through it; notwithstanding, the Silver Rule presents one of the truths of God. C. S. Lewis, in his fascinating book *The Abolition of Man,* makes the point that all the ethnic religions with their false gods nevertheless share some ethical concepts with Christianity. The failure of their adherents to live up to these concepts, even as those who profess Christianity do not live up to its precepts, brings them under the judgment of God. Were it not for the grace of God and the atoning death of Christ no man could be saved.

In our time the worst of all delusions is the one which deifies Satan and assigns to him attributes belonging to God alone. There are people today who are Satan worshippers, who have committed themselves completely to him. When men worship Satan they can slide no lower and their spiritual condition can get no worse. The eschatological beliefs of some Christians cause them to think that the increase in Satan worship is a definite sign of the end times. This may be true, but it is injudicious to be dogmatic. Paul sharply rebuked the Thessalonians for their misunderstanding at this point, declaring that the day of the Lord had not come and indeed would not come until other events, including the coming of the Anti-Christ, had first occurred. But even here the Christian should exercise the greatest of care. During World War II some mistakenly believed that Mussolini was the Anti-Christ.

Paul does say that "in later times" men will give heed "to deceitful spirits and doctrines of demons" (1 Tim. 4:1). John warns, "the rest of mankind . . . did not . . . give up worshipping demons . . . " (Revelation 9:20). We can only conclude that the choice is always between the one true God and some idolatrous substitute, including Satan. All substitutes are forbidden to men, who are called upon to love God and him alone.

The second commandment, which forbids graven images, follows hard on the first one and is organically related to it. At least two important points are connected with it, one having to do with the notion of who and what God is, and the other the ease with which men fall away from the first commandment.

The infinite, invisible God cannot be limited to plastic forms nor be truly represented in any man-made fashion. Graven images profess to give men some real idea of what God is like. This cannot be done; for if the whole world were filled with figures of God they would all give the wrong impression, and there would not be enough of them to begin to fill the need. God is a spirit, and any endeavor by man to anthropomorphize him does violence to his being and person. Such efforts end up humanizing God and bringing him down to the level of men. No artificial image, however conceived, has ever succeeded in lifting God above what he is or even come close to conveying his reality.

One of the great Scriptural truths about God is found in

the incarnation of Jesus Christ. He is the person who differs from all persons who ever lived or ever shall live. Jesus is the God-man; one person with two natures, human and divine. Men have always craved to see God; in Jesus Christ we do see him. But the incarnation has a soteriological thrust: Jesus came to take man's place, to die for his sins. Thus God has made himself known in history, not in the form of wood and stone, but in the unique person of Jesus, who could say, "He that hath seen me hath seen the Father" (John 14:9). Therefore no man can claim guiltlessness because God is invisible, a spirit without form. God has chosen to manifest himself physically in Jesus Christ. But note that it is in human form, not in wood or stone. Jesus, in human form, was thrust into the matrix of history and was able to demonstrate by what he said and how he lived that he was the true and living God. No man spoke or lived like this man, for no other man was ever sinless.

Now men do make statues to represent Jesus, his mother Mary, and the Apostles. All too often this leads to breaking the commandment against images. Churches have even differed on whether flat surface images are acceptable, while condemning those that are three-dimensional. This kind of battle itself is indicative of the dangers involved in the use of any representation of Jesus or Mary. Worshippers in some instances genuflect before such images. Some theologians rationalize that by saying that they bow to the person, not to the image which is only a representation. But the fine distinctions of the theologians sometimes escape the worshippers who invest the image with attributes it does not and cannot possess. In any event, the pagans made a similar defense of their practices which the early Christians condemned as idolatrous.

The ease with which men fall away from the commandment against graven images is amazing, springing, no doubt, from man's desire to see God through the eye. But strangely enough, in other areas of life men do not demand that they see everything in order to believe. The human eye does not see electricity. Nor do men demand to see it in order to believe in it or to avail themselves of its power. Love is not something that can be put under a microscope to measure its intensity and degree. In some ways its existence is shown by the acts of men, but many other motives can cause men to act in the same fashion that love can. Heroism, theatricals, pride, or even daredeviltry can lead a man to give his life for another.

Thought is another unseen and unmeasurable part of life. Its intricacies cannot be understood fully. For example, it is scientifically impossible to account for the wide range of different conclusions drawn by men having access to the same raw data. We cannot know the part emotions play in human decisions nor appreciate fully the roles of environment, sickness, or one's psychological orientation.

Some of these peculiarities can be seen in Communistic atheism, which is rationally ridiculous. The most that anyone can claim about the non-existence of God is agnosticism— to say you don't know. But as soon as one takes the atheist's viewpoint, he opens himself and his philosophical system to a dilemma. No finite being can say there is no God, for outside the limits of his knowledge God may exist. To be an atheist he must claim omniscience, which is to make himself a god. The Soviet Union professes materialism and denies the existence of God, but then humanistic substitutes are used to fill the need of the human heart for something to which to pay allegiance. One need only note the long parade of people in Moscow who pass by the bier of Lenin every day. This corpse has been lifted from its mortality to a place of immortality and invested with attributes that cause people to pay their respect to it. The Soviet Union has done for Lenin in death what the people of Rome did for their rulers in life. They deified them and gave them titles of the gods and made them objects of worship.

The second commandment exalts the uniqueness of the one true and living God and requires men to abstain from anything that would compromise this uniqueness, or become a substitute for him, or a rival to him. The commandment against graven images is a call to let God be God; when he is, nothing by way of thought, action, or image can come between the one who worships and the one who is worshipped.

The third commandment exalts the holiness, sacredness, and reverence men should have for the name of God. His name is not to be used in any derogatory fashion nor employed in any way that would bring dishonor upon it. The command is saying that we are to live in the awareness of God's existence. The name by which God is known is quite different from the names by which we are known. To misuse that name is to deny the primacy of the person whose name is violated. This means that the heart is not right. Multitudes of people carelessly say, "God damn it" who would never say, "Lindsell damn it" or "Washington damn it!" Using God's name in any way that hurts its holiness, lowers its value, or casts any shadow upon it is to do violence to his proclamation, "I am the Lord thy God."

It is commonplace for men to take oaths in the name of God. Thus, even when talking with friends or acquaintances, a man is apt to say, "I swear by the name of God that what I say is true." This calls God to witness to a man's veracity and lays a veneer over his words. Men swear by God because he is the greater, but whether Christians ought to do this is another matter. The Christian is commanded in the latter part of the Decalogue to speak the truth. What need is there for a Christian to swear by God's name that he is telling the truth? If he loves God, he will tell the truth and swearing by God's name becomes unnecessary. If he doesn't love God, then all the oaths in the world will not guarantee that he is telling the truth.

The name of Jesus Christ is most frequently taken in vain. There is no other name among men that is more abused. The true command is to use the names of God and Jesus Christ properly, with reverence and commitment. To call on those names for other purposes is to make God and Jesus Christ into something they are not and lessen the value of their names. If we love God the Father, we will love Jesus Christ the Son. And Jesus himself commands us to "love the Lord your God with all your heart, and with all your soul, and with all your mind" (Mt. 22:37). Is this not comprehensive, including the whole being of man? Heart, soul, and mind can mean nothing less than the all embracing, all comprehensive totality of life.

St. Augustine was right when he said, "Love God and do what you want." For when men love God they do what God wants, and one of the things God wants is for his name to be preserved spotless and without blemish in the hearts and on the tongues of those who say they love him.

The fourth commandment is quite affirmative. It tells us to keep the sabbath day holy (Ex. 20:8 ff.). What does this mean and what day does it refer to?

There are differing views about the sabbath which require a word. Some believe that the sabbath is a creation ordinance pre-dating the Mosaic law. Others believe it is part of the Mosaic economy. Some believe the sabbath commandment has been abolished under the New Testament dispensation, while others hold that it forever remains a part of the moral law of God; the idea of one day in seven for God and for rest and recreation is always valid. Some believe Saturday is the only biblically commanded day, while others hold that the first day of the week has taken its place.

So far as the New Testament evidence is concerned it

appears that Paul taught that one day is as good as another. In Colossians 2:16, 17 he charges that no one is to pass judgment on the believer "in questions of food and drink or with regard to a festival or a new moon or a sabbath. These are only a shadow of what is to come . . ." In Romans 14:5 he says, "One man esteems one day as better than another, while another man esteems all days alike. Let every one be fully convinced in his own mind. He who observes the day, observes it in honor of the Lord . . . " (vs. 5, 6).

It would appear to me that the sabbath principle is firmly entrenched in the Bible, and that the principle contained in the Ten Commandments remains forever true. I do not believe, on the basis of the Pauline teaching (and evangelicals generally believe in the unity of Scripture), that Saturday alone fulfills the requirements of the command. Nor do I believe that it necessarily need be Sunday. The principle is that one day in seven shall be set apart for God. When this injunction is followed, believers are indicating that God is the Lord of their lives and that they are in subordination and obedience to him.

The purpose of the sabbath is plain. It is not a private day, but is intended as a day for the worship of God and the fellowship of the saints. Of course, a church can make a work day of the Christian sabbath, with far too many meetings and far too much expenditure of energy. It was not only intended for the worship of God but also for the physical re-creation of man.

In the United States a form of legalism once attended the Christian sabbath, and Blue Laws were legislated in almost every community. But whatever legalism there was has now yielded to license. The Christian sabbath is wide open to every conceivable business enterprise, including stores, restaurants, and gasoline stations. Many Christians eat at restaurants, buy gasoline, and frequent the stores on Sunday, just as their unbelieving neighbors do. Sporting events, whether baseball, football, hockey, basketball, or golf, occur on Sunday. Television has further complicated the matter in bringing these events into the living rooms of both Christians and non-Christians.

The Christian sabbath is not a legislative problem. Surely no useful purpose would be served by requiring unbelievers to keep the sabbath commandment which Christians acknowledge. But the unhappy fact is that Christians (myself included) are more and more inclined to disregard the sabbath commandment through laxness and sloth, not to mention the ease with which we adopt the patterns of the world.

It is written in the laws of the universe that man shall work six days and set apart the seventh as a day of rest and worship. Christians who engage in activities forcing other people to work are hurting their neighbors whom they have been called upon to love. Christians have six days in the week in which to eat in restaurants; there is no pressing need for them to eat out on Sunday as well. They can fill their automobiles with gasoline on Saturday just as easily as on Sunday. All the groceries they need can be bought before Sunday; and even if they lacked some items, few Christians would suffer by fasting for a Sunday or two.

Jesus kept the sabbath and, according to the Jewish understanding of his day, broke it as well. But Jesus declared that the Son of man is Lord of the sabbath and that the sabbath was made for man, not man for the sabbath. The principle is clearly set forth in Scripture that works of necessity and mercy are permissible on the Christian sabbath. Jesus defended his disciples who plucked corn on the sabbath in order to satisfy their hunger (see Mt. 12:1 ff.). This was a work of necessity.

Immediately following in Matthew is the account of one of

Jesus' works of mercy, in which he healed a man with a withered hand. His enemies argued that he was performing work on the sabbath, and this was forbidden. Jesus knew, however, that they would save a dumb animal which had fallen into a pit on the sabbath. He asked whether a human being with a physical need was not equally worthy of mercy on the sabbath as a beast. Their answer was negative but Jesus held the other view.

It might be well to phrase it this way: Jesus held a high view of the sabbath; but he did not make it absolute. He acknowledged that there are exceptional circumstances based on works of necessity and mercy, which require an apparent breaking of the commandment. Let every man be free in his own heart to determine whether what he does falls into these categories. The Apostle Paul sums up the great truth of Christian freedom with a caution that should cause every believer to consider whether what he is doing is proper or improper. "So each of us shall give account of himself to God" (Rom. 14:12). We are not to judge one another; we are to allow others liberty. We are to remind one another that while we do not have to give an account to our brothers and sisters in the faith of what we do, we do have to give an account to God himself. And we had better come with clean hands and a pure heart when we face the Lord the judge.

The fifth commandment is the only one to which a specific promise is attached, although obedience to the whole law of God brings its blessings and the assurances of God's favor. The fifth commandment says: "Honor your father and your mother, that your days may be long in the land which the Lord your God gives you" (Ex. 20:12). Obviously this command, like the others, is addressed to the people of God. But we should remember that obedience to parents is written in general revelation and is almost universally practiced by worshippers in ethnic religions and by others as well. In Exodus the command is specially addressed to God's covenant people. There are few problems when this command is obeyed within the biblical context.

Christian parents will teach their children the commandments of God and bring them up in the nurture and admonition of the Lord. In all of this they will teach them that God intended for children to obey their parents in all things. At the same time, the parents will love their children, do only what is good for them, and require obedience in the Lord. In fact, fathers are told not to provoke their children even as children are told to obey their parents. When Christian parents and Christian children are committed to God and living according to God's ordinances there will be few problems. But this ideal condition does not always exist, and troubles do arise between parents and children. What to do then?

The first question has to do with the age of consent. When can children conclude they are no longer under the command to obey their parents? Or must they obey parents as long as they live? There is no doubt whatever that children are to honor their parents as long as their parents live. Nor is there any doubt that they are to care for their parents if necessary. Jesus gave the Pharisees rather rough treatment for their disregard of the commandment to care for their parents. It is important to note that the Pharisees did not deny their responsibility but shifted the emphasis, saying that by giving to God, the practice called corban, that which would have otherwise gone to the parents, they were not breaking the law. Jesus told them that they made the commandment void by the traditions of men. Children indeed are to care for their parents.

In our affluent society many elderly people are shunted off to rest homes and to retirement places simply because children do not wish to have their parents around or to accept personal responsibility; yet they are willing to accept financial responsibility for retirement accommodations. There are parents who wither on the vine of loneliness and suffer from the failure of children to give them moral, personal, and spiritual support by having them around the home. It is true that caring for elderly parents who get crotchety and sometimes senile in old age can be a problem. But raising children is also a problem, and Christians ought not abdicate their obligations to parents just because it requires time, patience, and thoughtfulness. Of course, if a parent reaches a point where home care is impossible there is no reason not to place him in a hospital or a home where treatment and professional help can be administered.

So far as children doing what their parents want them to do, this facet of the command has some normal built-in exceptions. If a child's parents are not Christian (or even if they are) and they demand that a child do what God has forbidden, the command does not apply. No child is required by God to steal because his parents tell him to do so. Nor should any girl submit to sexual advances by her father, or a boy to sexual advances made by his mother. This is incest and is forbidden.

God says that marriage makes a difference in obligations of filial obedience. In marriage a man leaves his mother and father and cleaves to his wife, and they become one flesh. In the establishment of their own homes children are freed from parental authority. They certainly should listen to the counsel and advice of their parents, and they should honor them. But they need not obey them. Roughly speaking, children should obey their parents so long as they remain under their roof.

Another specific problem arises when parents ask their children to do things that are not illicit, but which the children do not want to do. At this point Scripture seems clear that children who would honor God must honor their parents and do what they ask. This can be inconvenient and can cause hardship. One can adduce specific cases that would normally justify a child's refusal to obey at a particular point. But if the child cannot persuade his parents to see it his way, it seems clear enough that the decision of the parents is final. When children obey their parents they learn the lesson of obedience to God as well. Moreover, children can benefit from their parents' experience and often later realize how valuable it was for their elders to forbid them to do what they thought was good, but in reality was unwise. Obedience to parents also prepares young people for life. No one is free to do whatever he pleases. The child who learns obedience will more easily adapt himself to changing circumstances of life and not rebel against every frustration.

It would be foolish to suggest that parents are always right. But since they are older and have had more experience, it is not unlikely that they will be right more often than their children. I remember when one of my daughters expressed a desire to dance. It so happened that in our family dancing was not on the approved list of activities. She asked why she could not make her own decision, and adduced the fact that the children of one of my colleagues on the same faculty were given the privilege of making their own decision on this matter. When I inquired what she would do if she made her own decision, she replied promptly that she would attend the prom and dance. I replied that in this case I had to say no to her for the following reason: I acknowledged that I might be wrong in my decision, but that for me to let her do what I personally felt was wrong would be to abdicate my responsibility as her father. I would have loved to have said yes, but my convictions being what they were, I could not. She accepted the decision in a pouting fashion, but I doubt that any enduring damage was done to her psyche, nor do I think that her social life was impaired beyond remedy. At any rate she went to a college where there was no dancing, met a splendid young Christian man whom she married, established her own home, and still doesn't dance so far as I know. But if she were to choose to dance as a married woman, I would offer no objections and issue no commands. Nor would I tell her and her husband how they should raise their children concerning this issue about which the Scripture itself offers no precise guidance.

One of the dominant characteristics of conditions at the end times will be the disobedience of children to their parents. Disobedience seems to be on the increase among Western peoples, but it would be inaccurate as well as premature to say that the majority of young people are disobedient to their parents. Christian parents are sometimes responsible for the attitude of disobedience in their children because of their own lack of love, lack of concern, or lack of teaching their children the first principles of righteousness.

We now turn our attention from the positive, affirmative statements of the Ten Commandments to those and other prohibitions which might be thought of as negative. We should approach them, however, with the thought in mind that for those who love God with their whole hearts the prohibitions are not grievous, nor does keeping them involve taking away anything that is really worthwhile.

VI. LYING, COVETING, STEALING
AND KILLING

In laying the groundwork for the discussion of ethical and moral conduct, mention was made of contextual or situation ethics popularized by Fletcher in his book *Situation Ethics*. The extent to which the principles espoused by him and many others have found their way into Protestant denominational life, particularly in the sexual area, must be noted.

At the meeting in 1970 of the General Assembly of the United Presbyterian Church, U.S.A., a report on human sexuality was received for study by the Commissioners of the Church. Louis Cassels of the United Press International wrote a column on the methodology of commissions appointed to study controversial subjects. Their reports are submitted, he said, but it is then asserted that they are not officially approved positions of the church. Meanwhile the unbiblical positions expressed in these reports become the practice of church officialdom, even while those who protest are assured that these are not "official." Cassels called this hypocrisy, and severely criticized those who bring into their church, by devious means, what they can not get accepted by straightforward, honest methods. Ironically, a motion made on the floor of the General Assembly affirming that the Old Testament and the New Testament do in fact label fornication, adultery, and homosexuality sin was passed by such a small margin that if five affirmative votes had been changed the motion would have been lost. In its 1970 meeting, the Lutheran Church of America had to deal with a similar report, and the methodology was much the same as that of the United Presbyterian Church.

The point here is not that a few denominations (for there have been others) have introduced unbiblical notions concerning sexual conduct, although this has been the case, but that in their practice of contextual ethics they are saying that the end justifies the means. Many Christians are considered old-fashioned thinkers who must be educated to accept and practice what is presently rejected. Since church members generally balk at a clearly presented issue of this type calling for a definite decision, the avant garde advocates of the new morality resort to means to hide their true intentions, including deceit, trickery, and outright lying. This is nothing more or less than hypocrisy—pretending to be what one is not in order to make people think something other than the truth.

What is really at stake here is the ninth commandment, "Thou shalt not bear false witness against thy neighbor" (Exodus 20:16). To be a hypocrite, whether by pretending to be what one is not, or by speaking what is not true, is to be a liar. This introduces, of course, the vital question of whether a lie is ever justifiable. According to contextual ethics it is. If a lie is told in love and for the alleged good of the person involved, it is not only permissible but obligatory.

When giving examples of lies, the proponents of the lie usually do three things. First, they take for illustration the kind of incident that either never happens or is so rare that virtually no one is ever faced with one of that kind. Second, they usually include in the illustration a secondary element which makes the person involved forced to choose the lesser of two undesirable alternatives and be guilty of a still greater sin if he does not tell a lie. Third, their illustration is used to evoke a deep sympathetic response to make those who do not respond affirmatively appear heartless. The classic illustration, of course, is that of the man who has hidden Jews in his cellar. Nazi soldiers appear at his door and ask him if he has any Jews in his house. If he answers in the negative he has told a lie. If he responds in the affirmative he seems to have no heart and can be held responsible, so they say, for the deaths of all the Jews in his cellar. Using this premise, one might then reason that the person identifying the gunman who has just killed a policeman then becomes responsible for the death of the gunman when the jury sends him to the gas chamber. These conclusions do not follow, but they act as psychological conditioners to make a person feel that telling a lie in some cases is justifiable.

Certainly God knew what he was doing when he forbade lying. A lie is not only a breach that offends God's holiness but it is also destructive of personal well-being, making open, honest, and enduring interpersonal relationships difficult if not impossible. The man who knows his friend will lie to him at times he thinks good and appropriate to do so, can never be sure when his friend will tell him the truth. He will always have to ask himself whether this time he is being deceived. His friend's wife can have no enduring certainty of her husband's truthfulness, nor can his children ever be sure their father will not deceive them. His business associates soon learn to view his words with skepticism. No matter how seriously the liar defends his position the unbelieving world rightly laughs at his Christian profession, for it knows, even if he doesn't, that lying belongs to the world, not to the believer. The world indeed expects the Christian to tell the truth and to act with integrity because the world itself has standards with respect to truth. If by the judgment of the world a man is a fraud and a hoax, what will he be in the sight of God before whom he shall stand in the judgment?

There is still another aspect that should not be overlooked. When one man lies in order to manipulate another's decisions, he defaces the image of God in the one he deceives. The liar takes to himself prerogatives belonging to the person he lies to, and even though the liar thinks it is for the person's good, he deprives him of his selfhood, his right to choose, and the right to be responsible for and bear the consequences of his own decision. He is playing God in the life of the man he lies to, and this is serious business. It is a role that does not belong to mere humans and can only damage both parties in the end. Because lying is close to the heartbeat of the world, the Christian should make every effort to glorify God by telling the truth.

COVETOUSNESS

Another arrow in the quiver of worldliness is expressed in the tenth commandment, "Thou shalt not covet." Lying deep in the fabric of personal and national life, its corporate as well as personal implications make coveting a considerable force in international as well as in interpersonal relations. Few Christians realize that coveting is a root from which other sins, including many wars, spring. Stealing is preceded by coveting, by wanting what somebody else owns. Fornication is preceded by coveting the sexual rights of the other person. Adultery is preceded by coveting somebody else's wife or husband. King David was far removed from any sudden, overwhelming, and uncontrollable desire for Bathsheba. He saw her from his rooftop and coveted her, knowing she was the wife of Uriah the Hittite, one of his faithful soldiers. He summoned Bathsheba to his presence with one thought in mind, that of seducing her. Yet the adultery which followed was not his responsibility alone.

Bathsheba did not have to come when he summoned her. She knew what she was headed for when she obeyed. David got not only what he coveted, but more than he bargained for: he became a murderer. For all of these sins the judgment of God fell on him (cf. 2 Sam. 11, 12).

Virtually all theft is based upon the desire to take what belongs to someone else. It is a sin in itself, however, even when not leading to the actual deed. Men covet many things which they do not obtain, but failure to obtain them does not relieve them of the guilt of the desire nor shield them from the psychologically damaging effects of always wanting what someone else has.

Envy, which is another aspect of coveting, is directed to individuals, and is manifested in a variety of ways. Your friend has a Cadillac while you have a Ford; you covet the Cadillac and envy your friend. A fellow minister has a big church while you have a small one; you covet his congregation and envy the minister. A man has a great singing voice but you have none; yet you would like a voice similar to his. Some friend has a substantial home while you have a modest one; you want one like his or better, and you envy him and his possession. Perhaps what someone else has is a status symbol, and what you really covet is the status it brings. Maybe you think, "I'm a better man than he and better qualified for the job he holds." This thought is both envious and covetous.

There are probably few evangelists who have not watched Billy Graham with green eyes of jealousy. How they would like to stand before multiplied thousands of people and watch large numbers move forward to receive Christ for the glory of God, but with envy as a motivating force. Surely thousands of ministers have felt they could preach better sermons than Billy Graham, and some may do so without getting the same response. Is there not lurking behind even this, the demon of envy, the sin of coveting, and jealousy?

If you scratch beneath the surface deep enough you will find it buried there despite every disclaimer.

Is not name dropping another form of covetousness? Since you have not been able to attain what you covet, you try to gain it vicariously by identifying yourself (and I myself) with someone who has attained. Perhaps you are among those who say: "Oh, yes, Mr. Nixon is a personal friend of mine." Or, "I knew so and so when he wasn't what he is today." In the first instance you build your own status and fulfill your own envy by identifying with the person and his accomplishments; in the second instance you demean the other fellow to show you knew him when he wasn't something great. But even here you are expressing your envy of what he has become and desire for what you would like to be. Envy and covetousness are marks of the worldling, not marks of the Christian. For the Christian to be caught up in these is to be *of* the world as well as *in* the world. Covetousness does not have the marks of Calvary connected with it. No one knows this better than Satan himself, because the first sin was not overt disobedience but covetousness, a lusting after what God was and had. Satan envied God, and wanted to be like the most high; he did not want to imitate God but wanted to be God. Covetousness, whether coming through the flesh and its physical appetites or through the imagination, is high on Satan's list of fiery darts which all too often pierce us to our undoing as believers who are called to be in the world but not of it.

STEALING

In the believer's battle against the world's temptations it would be easy to glide by the eighth commandment, "Thou shalt not steal," either because few Christians are guilty of its grosser forms or because they are sometimes unaware of what constitutes theft. Ordinarily the adulterer doesn't think he is a thief. But in fact he has stolen his neighbor's wife. Thus he is guilty of covetousness, of adultery, and of stealing. Most Christians would be horrified at the thought of snatching a purse, holding up a bank, or robbing a supermarket. They would not steal a car or falsify the accounts of their employers; yet a man who steals a penny is just as guilty as the one who purloins a million dollars. Quantitatively there may be a vast difference but qualitatively they are the same crime. Wherein lies the difference, if any?

As a good psychologist and a fine student of human nature, Satan is fully aware of human idiosyncrasies and how to deal with them. He knows that even Christians are apt to gloss over petty thievery as inconsequential, while at the same time waxing indignantly righteous over large scale larceny. So he tempts them to petty thievery, giving them cause to justify it, or at least to rationalize it. But stealing is stealing, whether explained away, made to appear innocuous, or overlooked as a mere trifle. The small, apparently innocent, lump in the flesh may veil what will become a horrible and extensive malignancy if not cut out and removed in the earliest stages. What are some of those innocent looking lumps that are easily overlooked?

Anyone who works in a large office is tempted to petty pilfering, which may involve only a lead pencil costing a nickel or the company stamp used on a personal letter; the personal phone call that wasn't paid for, or the padded expense account. Maybe you bought something for which you were undercharged and did nothing about it, or received and kept more change than was coming to you. A very small and apparently inconsequential pebble, when left in a shoe, shortly produces a big blister on the foot. No one ought to forget the well-known moral: For the want of a nail a shoe was lost; for the want of a shoe a horse was lost; for the want of a horse a man was lost; for the want of the man a kingdom was lost. There is no such thing as an insignificant theft.

The purpose here is not to make a legalist of anyone, hard as that may be. Most Christians seem to prefer antinomianism in order to sin that grace may abound. Rather, the design is to create a sensitivity toward right perspective and action. Sin has a way of growing in and desensitizing most people: what they once shunned they embrace; what they once hated they love; what they once did with loathing they do without a tremor or a pang of guilt.

How easy it is to fail to count all the strokes on the golf course, to cheat in the game when the other fellow isn't looking. "Let him that stole, steal no more" (Eph. 4:28), and if he, like Zacchaeus, has "taken anything from any man by false accusation," let him "restore him fourfold" (Luke 19:8).

KILLING

A close second to the abuse of sex today is the new and unexpected twist which has come into vogue concerning killing. Whereas standards of sexuality, morality, and honesty have been loosened considerably, even among so-called Christians, the opposite is true regarding killing. Many inveigh against it while taking a light view of sexual escapades, the use of drugs, and smoking pot. Capital punishment has virtually ceased to exist in America and many other countries. More and more young people say they are opposed to war, and perhaps at no time in the twentieth century have more of them been opposed to a particular war than that which was waged in Vietnam. Opponents have called it immoral, murderous, and a blot on America's name.

The fact that resistance to killing seems to be a movement in the opposite direction from loosening standards in most other matters is no necessary index of the rightness or

wrongness of killing. Indeed, those who embrace situation
ethics would be the first to admit that killing is sometimes
necessary, but even among them some of the loudest voices
have been raised against it. The illogic of it all does not
seem to impress them. Moreover, those who oppose killing
and simultaneously stand outside the Christian faith are
among the most moralistic on this point. Clearly, in order
to label something immoral, some view of morality must be
held first, against which to gauge immorality. And if all
morality is time-conditioned and relative, then killing cannot
be ruled out on a moral basis.

The Christian, however, claims to adhere to biblical revelation and professes to follow its teachings. What then does
the Bible teach about killing? Is there an absolute prohibition against it or are exceptions made? For the moment
our main concern is with war, capital punishment, and killing
by private individuals of robbers, rapists, etc. In the next
chapter, following the discussion on sex, we will consider
abortion. Theoretically, abortion can be considered either
under the heading of killing or in relation to sex. I have
chosen to discuss abortion in the chapter dealing with sex
for two reasons: first, without sexual union there can be no
conception leading to abortion. Second, the biblical evidence
having to do with this subject relates specifically to human life
subsequent to gestation and not life in the womb. Just as
Scripture is silent about the use of drugs, although propound-
ing relevant principles from which a viewpoint may be
adduced, so it does not afford much light specifically on abortion. This could, without doubt, be considered under the
section on killing, but the writer's choice is to discuss it as
part of the sexual life of the Christian.

Having said this, the preeminent question requiring consideration and an answer is: is it ever right to kill someone
deliberately by choice rather than by accident?

The commandment, "Thou shalt not kill," has been misunderstood by many people. It would be better stated, "Thou shalt not commit murder." The distinction between murder and killing is fairly clear. In criminal law, first degree murder must include prior intention and malice. In second degree murder there is no premeditation. A drunken man who kills another man in a brawl without prior intent is guilty of second degree murder. If one man kills another in self defense he is not guilty of murder at all, nor is a workman who accidentally drops a bucket of tar from the roof of a building, killing a passerby. The Scripture clearly forbids murder but does not thereby regard all taking of life as murder.

There is no doubt that the Old Testament provides for both capital punishment and killing in wartime. This is so obvious that one need not belabor it. Genesis 9:6 says, "Whoso sheddeth man's blood, by man shall his blood be shed." Moses commanded capital punishment for, among other things, murder, kidnapping, cursing one's father or mother (Exod. 21:12 ff.), adultery, and for intercourse with an animal (Deut. 20:10, 15, 16). Moreover, God commanded the Israelites to slay their enemies in war. Saul was told to kill all of the Amalekites, and his incomplete obedience lost him his kingdom and his crown (1 Sam. 15:3 ff.). God himself slew the Egyptian soldiers in the Red Sea. From this it is fair to say that those who executed capital punishment or engaged in killing in warfare were not guilty of murder.

Having established the fact that killing was permissible, and indeed at times commanded in the Old Testament, it does not follow that what was laid down in the Old Testament is automatically true for the New Testament, since many Old Testament practices were cancelled out or superseded in the New Testament. What, then, is the New Testament teaching about killing?

For hundreds of years Christian pacifists have been a minority who have numbered among their adherents Quakers and various kinds of Mennonites. Some Christians in the larger denominations have been pacifists, even though no large denomination has ever adopted an official pacifist position. Pacifism is an absolutist view, which considers killing wrong, not just war alone. To kill someone in self-defense is wrong; to kill a man to prevent him from raping any woman is wrong. The pacifist view solves all problems neatly with no irritating difficulties about just and unjust wars or occupations such as policeman or soldier.

Christian pacifism (or non-resistance) is based on the teaching of Jesus to love your enemy, holding that the New Testament advocates non-violence and that therefore the Old Testament is superseded. What it has no legitimacy to do is to use the commandment "Thou shalt not kill" as substantive grounds for pacifism. Moreover, this position fails to deal adequately with the Pauline teaching about the office of the magistrate and his sword-bearing responsibility (see, e.g., Romans 13). Paul said he was willing to die if he had broken any Roman law that made him worthy of death—a strange statement if he was a pacifist, because he then should have argued that he could not be put to death for any reason.

Those who are not pacifists face many and varied problems. In his vocation as a soldier, or when military service is required by his government, a man may be called upon to kill in the line of duty. This is not murder. But this apparently simple conclusion is complicated by another factor that enters the case, having to do with the definition of just and unjust wars.

During the period of the early church it does not appear that Christians went to war. Certainly for the first several hundred years Christian communities did not constitute nations with kings and armies, and the problem of war and peace for the nation calling itself Christian did not arise. Moreover, church history affords instances of soldiers who, when they became Christians, left the military. Some of them died for doing so. The time did come, however, when Christian theologians wrestled with the problem of whether it was ever justifiable for a Christian to wage war.

For hundreds of years Christian conscience has approved of war in principle, justifying this conclusion on the basis that there are just and unjust wars. It has not sanctified unjust wars nor concluded that Christians should wage them. But has there ever been a just war? Are there not two sides to every war, and has not the nation that has been attacked often provided sufficient provocation for the aggressor? Does the individual Christian have the right to determine whether a war is indeed justified, or should he be obedient to his government's decision to wage war? The matter is further complicated when we ask questions about the responsibility of nations to assist other and perhaps weaker nations which have been attacked by more powerful ones. We need to be specific about this.

The United States went to war against Germany, Italy, and Japan in World War II. But before the United States entered the war many other nations were already engaged in the conflict. Britain earlier had tried the policy of appeasement with Hitler. Chamberlain went to Munich and bought what he called "peace in our time." But his capitulation did not assuage Hitler. The Germans and their Soviet allies invaded Poland, which the British had a pact to assist in case of attack. Two questions arise. Should the British ever have signed an agreement to rescue Poland if it were attacked? Should the British, when Poland was attacked, have come to its aid when unprepared militarily and when doing so would mean an extension of the war and the beginning of a world conflict?

The British went to war against Germany to fulfill their treaty obligations. But they also went to war because they felt that Hitler was a threat to Britain. Their own national interests were at stake as well. In other words, self-interest was a component in the decision to wage war. Any objective observer would have to admit that Hitler, a madman, had embarked on a course of conquest that could be stopped only by military force. The United States threw its weight on the side of the democracies against the three totalitarian powers. The exigencies of the war, however, forced the democracies to accept the help of an equally totalitarian power, the Soviet Union, who joined the military alliance. War makes strange bedfellows.

Undoubtedly justice and equity in World War II were on the side of the democracies in their decision to wage war against Hitler and his allies. If there is such a thing as a just war, this was one. But this opinion was not shared by all, including perhaps some Christians. What, then, does the Christian do when his own conscience is violated by a war he cannot justify, even though most Christians agree that it is a just war? The answer is plain enough from Scripture. The Christian has a prior allegiance to God and to his kingdom. If he believes a war to be unjust, whatever the opinion of other Christians may be, he ought not to fight.

Whoever decides against entering the military during what he terms an unjust war should remember two things: (1) he can be wrong and the other Christians right; therefore he is not free to pass final judgment on those who do wage war; (2) he who refuses to kill (and the pacifist or non-resister must be included as well) may still be an accessory before, during, or after the fact, and thus be guilty of killing even when he has not fired a shot or dropped a bomb.

The man who manufactures, sells, distributes, transports, or otherwise has dealings in military or non-military goods used in war also has a responsibility. The farmer whose wheat feeds soldiers is implicated. Even the man who does nothing more than pay taxes, which in turn are used to support the military machine, cannot escape involvement.

We ought not settle for answers based upon a war that was relatively easy to justify; rather, we should consider a difficult and vexing war like Viet Nam. This is no easy task because most people are emotionally involved in this issue and react with more heat than light. For ten years the United States was subjected to constant and steadily increasing criticism by those in the United States and around the world who opposed the war as a moral issue. Some of the objections were based upon sincere and credible foundations; others were mere propaganda used skillfully and expeditiously by Communist countries against the world's leading capitalist nation. Historians will require years to untangle the facts and render any kind of reliable judgment. In the trauma of the death of John F. Kennedy historical judgments were rendered widely which, a decade later, are being subjected to closer scrutiny and increasingly being shown to have been erroneous. The Camelot of the Kennedy days is giving way to the realism of the facts distorted in the aftermath of the assassination.

It seems clear that the United States got into the war in Viet Nam because it felt that the Communist North would overrun South Viet Nam and all of southeast Asia, and that the worldwide interests of the United States would be damaged if this were allowed to happen. A further complication was the notion that the SEATO agreement included an obligation to defend peoples who were attacked by aggressors. Whether this should have applied to a civil war is another question. But the fact is that the North Vietnamese not only attacked South Viet Nam but also ravaged Laos and Cambodia and threatened Thailand. On the basis of self-interest, the preservation of balance of power, containment of Communism, and treaty obligations, the United States made a pragmatic decision to enter the war. Whether this was wise or not is another question.

Christian young men facing military service and being called upon to kill could not possibly wait for the historians' verdict in 1980 but had to make their decisions at that moment, based upon the information they had at hand. They could not wait to see whether this was a just or an unjust war. Bombarded with propaganda both for and against involvement, what were they to do? Not pacifists or believers in non-resistance, and accepting the notion of a just war, their problem was whether the Viet Nam war fit this description. Obviously, this or that individual cannot determine national policy, nor will any nation have policies which do not run counter to the Christian ethic. But the Christian cannot cop out by turning to physical separation from the world. This is contrary to Christ's teaching when he sent us to be light to the world.

In the case of whether or not to fight in Viet Nam, the decision for the Christian had to be an individual one based on the best information he had at the time. If the decision was that the war was unjust, he did not then have the option many non-Christian young men had of avoiding the draft by flight or by deception, of refusing to obey the law of the land and seeking to escape the corresponding penalties. When Caesar's law conflicts with God's law, according to the Christian's conscience, he should willingly accept the penalty of disobeying Caesar's law. The idea that a man is free to run away from the consequences of breaking a law because he thinks it is unjust can lead only to anarchy, in which every man does what is right in his own eyes. Anarchy is antithetical to Christian conscience. Jesus and the apostles subjected themselves to the laws of men for conscience's sake.

The highlight in modern history validating the principle

of personal responsibility came in the Nuremberg trials. Man after man pleaded not guilty on the grounds that he was merely obeying orders. But the judges determined that there are orders given by superiors that must be disobeyed. No man had a right to kill Jews in a gas chamber simply because he was ordered to do so by Hitler. He had only the right to disobey such an order and suffer the consequences. As it happened, many Germans escaped the wrath of Hitler only to experience the wrath of international justice later. It is sad that human beings should be called upon to face decisions in which they are likely to suffer whether they obey or disobey. But it is better to suffer for having made the right decision than to suffer for having made the wrong one.

We cannot leave this subject without referring to other morally ambiguous situations also involving the problem of war. Years ago the Soviet Union absorbed the Baltic States by sheer aggression and overwhelming brute force. Nobody is doing anything about them or their oppression. In more recent times the Soviet Union subjugated Hungary and Czechoslovakia, efforts which, unlike the war in Viet Nam, were not protracted. The Soviet Union applied such overwhelming force that the issue was decided quickly. Now both of these countries lie under the iron heel of dictatorship, their freedom gone. The United States, which entered the war in Viet Nam to help the South Vietnamese keep their freedom, did nothing in a military sense to assist either Hungary or Czechoslovakia. Should it have done so?

The lesson the Christian learns from incidents like these is a profound one. He realizes that there are injustices he cannot correct, abuses he cannot stop, limitations to his own powers and to the powers of the nation in which he lives. There are two things the Christian can do in situations like these: he can talk to the issues and try by moral persuasion to bring about change, and he can pray and ask the sovereign God of the universe to do something about these things. The option is also open to use force by subsidizing and encouraging revolution in the subjugated countries. But is this truly a Christian option? And if it is, can the Christian use this method selectively?

The question about selectivity is asked because it concerns a problem about which many Christians are divided. One of the characteristics of the leaders of the ecumenical movement is their justifiable and urgent concern for social justice. They are among the most vocal critics of Rhodesia, South Africa, Mozambique (and the Portuguese), Spain, Greece, and leaders of what they call the "forces of oppression" in Latin America. The United States is also the object of their criticism, albeit for a different reason. The World Council of Churches is the spearhead of the ecumenical movement, basing this outreach on the example of the Old Testament prophets, and going so far as to countenance violent revolution as the means by which to effect change. The World Council of Churches has given hundreds of thousands of dollars to revolutionary movements in South Africa and is advocating revolution in Latin America. Its bureaucrats approve of the Chilean regime and its expropriation of foreign properties. All of this is done in the name of the Church and on the presupposition that this is the true mission of the Church (of which we shall have something to say later on).

Now there is a vast difference between churches starting wars and revolutions, and differentiating between just and unjust wars they had no part in starting. But what is most frustrating is the unfairness of the World Council of Churches in selecting what causes to endorse. Yet this selectivity points up the fact of a calculated program designed to favor one kind of group over against another. No one can deny that Portuguese colonialism in Africa is shameful or that the whites of South Africa and Rhodesia are a minority who oppress the Negro; nor can one deny that Spain lies under the rule of a dictator, nor that the few landowners and the very wealthy of Latin America control the destinies of millions of downtrodden peasants, peons, and Indians.

Yet at the same time the Soviet Union, with its Central Committee and small 14.5 million party members, controls the lives of more than two hundred million Soviets plus millions of conquered peoples. Right now the Central Committee is purging the ranks of the party members to eliminate the unworthy and to boost Communist efficiency. Translated, this means consolidating the ranks of those who are the oppressors in order to keep the oppressed in line. Of all the evil in the world today none is greater than Communism; yet the so-called prophetic voice of the World Council of Churches wages no campaign to gain for Solzhenitsyn his right to freedom of speech as one who has confessed the Christian faith, gives no money to support the thousands of Baptist Christians who are being sent to Siberia all the time, does nothing to free the Czechs, Hungarians, Poles, Lithuanians, and others from the tyrannous yoke of Soviet oppression.

The point is clear that the Christian must not be selective in addressing himself to evil in the world. The enormity of what the Soviet Union has done and is doing, as well as the force it has exerted in military conquest, must be condemned. This does not mean that non-Communist evil should be spared criticism, for justice is blind and the scales are not weighted in favor of one sinner over against another. Whatever is of Satan must be opposed, and whatever is of God must be supported.

War and killing are not the whole story. Nations can secure their objectives by other means than armed force. It is an old cliché that when the diplomacy fails the matter is turned over to the military. But diplomacy is usually nothing more than an iron fist encased in a soft glove. Diplomacy has force only when backed by military might or by moral power with military force behind it. The lesson taught us by Hitler, who was only moved by considerations of military might, should suffice. He laughed at the diplomacy of the democracies, for it was a soft glove covering a sick fist. Worldwide moral indignation, unless also backed by the threat of force, will not stop a madman.

Besides diplomacy, nations wield economic power. The conduct of war today depends on an adequate supply of raw materials. No nation is self-sufficient but depends on other nations for help. What nations do for one another can make all the difference in the world, even the difference of survival. In 1972 the weather gave the Soviet Union a terrific jolt, causing it to suffer widespread crop failure. There was not enough grain to feed everyone. India also suffered grain shortages and its populace was threatened with starvation. The nations with surplus grain had these countries in their grip. A refusal to sell or give them grain would have resulted in human suffering on a vast scale. The biblical injunction to feed your enemy was deep in the consciousness of nations with many Christians among their populations. But a willingness by the United States to supply the Soviet Union with grain was also the occasion to force the Soviet Union to change its stance on the war in Viet Nam by using grain as bait. Added to this was the fact that the United States had a large balance of payments deficit, and the sale of domestic wheat to a foreign consumer would alleviate this situation also.

Sometimes small nations with raw materials that cannot be secured easily can influence world events. Rhodesia is a prime producer of chromium, with the Soviet Union the other large supplier of this commodity. The United States needs large supplies of chromium for its industries. If Rhodesian chromium is not available, the supply and demand is such that the Soviet Union can afford to charge high prices and control the market. But if Rhodesian chromium is available the economic situation is changed. Part of the reason why the United States has not fully observed the United Nations sanctions to Rhodesia has to do with this very fact. At one of the 1968 sessions of the World Council of Churches in Uppsala, Lord Caradan of Britain stated that the British could apply sanctions to Rhodesia but not to South Africa, with which Britain has such substantial trade relations, because to do so would bankrupt Britain. Thus economics is another form of war which sometimes leads to open hostility as well as averts it.

Whether a Christian is a pacifist or accepts the notion of just wars, the Bible leaves us with the last word. Jesus told us there will always be wars and rumors of wars (Matt. 24:6). These will come because of man's innate sinfulness. Christians are called upon to do all they can to keep nations from waging wars. They will never be able to introduce a warless world, but they may be able to stop them for a longer space of time. Wars are always caused by sin, but nations sometimes must wage war in response to sinful aggression.

In the end times God himself through Jesus Christ will fight against the devil and his armies. The justice and outcome of this last war will never be in doubt, leading to a just and an endless peace in which men shall beat their swords into ploughshares and their spears into pruning hooks to learn war no more (Rev. 19:11 ff.; Micah 4:3).

VII. SEX, ABORTION, AND PORNOGRAPHY

Christianity is not a legalistic faith, although some have made it appear so by their extensive prohibitions. Jesus condemned the legalism of the Pharisees, who enlarged upon the law of God by adding innumerable prohibitions which left one bound, harried, and virtually freedomless. These joyless religious fanatics and conscientious snoopers into other people's lives made existence miserable, even while simultaneously using the law to feather their own nests and relieve themselves of burdens they wanted others to bear. For example, the Pharisees defined the injunction against work on the Sabbath so narrowly that a man could travel only so far on that day without breaking the commandment. Jesus was accused of violating the law because he performed miracles of healing on the Sabbath. Even the tithe was defined down to the mint leaves and cummin, a dwarf plant grown for its aromatic leaves.

The solution to legalism is not to become antinomian. The addition long ago of an infinite number of needless prohibitions does not mean that Christians today are free to do whatever they please. They are only free to do the will of God. There are some prohibitions intrinsic to the life style of the Christian, some things which the Bible clearly and openly forbids. First and foremost the Mosaic law, with its injunctions which are repeated, enlarged, and clarified in the New Testament, forbids the making of graven images (Exodus 20:1 ff.). This is not so much a problem now as it was in a day when most men made idols. However, God also forbids blasphemy, or taking his name in vain. This is a universal problem which is not limited to the spoken word, but includes the thought life as well. As a man thinks in his heart, so is he (Prov. 23:7). To profane God's name in thought, as well as in word, is to break this commandment.

ADULTERY AND FORNICATION

The Seventh Commandment is "Thou shalt not commit adultery." This common sin involves sexual intercourse by a married person with someone to whom he or she is not married. Adultery also occurs in remarriage following a divorce for reasons other than sexual infidelity. It is condoned and its implications are overlooked by some evangelicals and fundamentalists who strongly attest to the authority of the Bible in doctrines such as the virgin birth, but who discount it concerning adultery. The adulterer can be forgiven and restored by God, but the sin is still gross and wretchedly wicked, impairing the beauty and unity of the marriage relationship and striking at the institution of the home. It harms the children of the marriage, can produce illegitimate offspring, and introduces a cancer into the life. Special havoc is wrought in the life of the innocent partner whose trust has been betrayed and whose relationship with the guilty spouse has been damaged for life, even though the marriage itself may not end in divorce. Adultery cannot be justified under any circumstances nor be shown to produce a greater good. To argue that the end justifies the means in this or any other sinful act is to make a liar of God and a saint of the devil.

Jesus took this commandment seriously and chose deliberately to discuss its implications. He made known that adultery does not overtake a man by force nor seize him suddenly, but is preceded by the sin of covetousness arising in the heart. Before adultery is ever committed by a man, the heart capitulates to coveting the woman. Jesus therefore says that heart adultery always precedes the physical act, but he does not say that the desire should be followed by the physical act nor that the one is the equivalent of the other. Spiritual adultery should be confessed and repented of, however, before it leads to its more obvious expression. In adultery, one person usually makes the advances to which the other yields. The seducer is more guilty than the one who submits, but the latter can never rightly claim complete helplessness. Whoever chooses to resist may become the victim of rape, but this is a different crime in which the victim either can be innocent or partly guilty.

It should be remembered that the commandment against adultery, as do other forbidden acts to be discussed, pertains only to those who place themselves under the rule of the law of God. The unbeliever is "free" to sin, but he must be warned that even for him there is guilt and judgment at the hands of the God he spurns. Legally, adultery is not recognized as a crime by most governments. This protects the adulterer from civil penalties for a spiritual offense. But such legal acceptability and absence of penalties should have no bearing on the actions of the believer, who lives according to the law of God in addition to the civil and criminal statutes of men.

Divorce due to adultery was no problem in the Old Testament: both partners in crime were stoned to death. Thus the marriage tie was broken by death, and the innocent party was then free to remarry. Since in most societies today adulterers are not put to death, one may logically conclude that divorce, followed by the remarriage of the innocent party, is quite appropriate if that person is really innocent (see here Matt. 19:3-12).

But what about the adulterer whose partner has divorced him, and who may now face the problem of sexual desire? He is then placed in the position of sinning if he remarries, and burning with lust if he doesn't. Is there no hope for him? This is a difficult situation, the answer to which depends upon the spiritual condition of the adulterer. If he is truly penitent, understands the seriousness of his offense, and resolves to live as a Christian, then it would appear the lesser of two evils for him to enter a new marriage relationship. If such a person remarries, without the consent of the church, in a civil ceremony he certainly should be denied access to the Lord's Table, unless and until the church is thoroughly satisfied that he is entitled to it.

Fornication, like adultery, is forbidden by God, although the decalogue does not single it out specifically. Both adulterers and fornicators are named in the New Testament among those who are excluded from God's kingdom (1 Cor. 6:9). The question today is whether premarital sex among believers is forbidden even when accompanied by love and perhaps the intention of marriage, and not engaged in simply for physical gratification; whether, in fact, premarital sex is ever legitimate. Again it is well to remember that the decision here should be based not on the notions of men but on the revelation of God. The Bible does not equivocate about fornication. It not only does not endorse it; it forbids it. The Bible is not anti-sex. God endorses sexual fulfillment and does not capriciously dangle alluring possibilities before his people which he then denies them. He is saying that sex, which is good, must be understood within a larger framework, not as a mere end in itself. Most animals engage in sexual activity as a result of a physiological reaction triggered by the female going into heat. The male responds instinctively, not rationally. However, man is human and differs from animals because he has the power of choice. He can forego sex temporarily or permanently for various reasons.

God has ordained that sexual fulfillment be relationally oriented. This means that what is legitimate, lovely, and fulfilling in one relationship is illegitimate, unlovely, and debasing in another. God has limited sex to marriage, and therefore has forbidden any premarital and extra-marital manifestations of it. These violate the unity of the sexes found only in marriage, produce trauma and lead to undesirable results that can never be known fully in advance. The laws of life are arrayed against it. Like the man who drives his car down a one-way street the wrong way, it leads to catastrophe. Scripture teaches that sexual intercourse causes two people to become one flesh (1 Cor. 6:16), and pictures this relationship as comparable to that of Jesus Christ the bridegroom to his Church the bride, to whom he is linked forever. The fornicator is spiritually ineffectual because he is repudiating his true relationship to Jesus Christ.

No argument can be advanced to justify fornication that could not have been used by Adam and Eve to justify eating the forbidden fruit in the Garden of Eden. And even when every conceivable argument has been postulated to justify premarital sex, the one unassailable and unchanging fact remains: the negative command of God. For the committed Christian this ought to be enough, even though he may not understand completely the reason for it. Moreover, there is much to be gained by remaining continent. All men are physical beings and thus have strong physical desires. The true mettle of a man is tested by his ability to control his passions rather than by the ability of his passions to control him. Satan encourages a false liberty which is in reality license, for he knows that one of the gateways to hell is illicit sex and that it always results in spiritual backsliding and in living as a worldling. History affords no example of any great leader who has generated spiritual power while in thralldom to either adultery or fornication.

Abortion, like the misuse of sex, is no newcomer to the contemporary scene. It simply seems one in an age already marked by great permissiveness, in which Christians and the Church, spurred by concern over world over-population, have bent the law of God to sociological, economic, and political considerations. At stake is the Sixth Commandment, "Thou shalt not kill." This commandment, as we have seen in the last chapter, forbids murder. In the previous discussion on this subject we deliberately left out abortion for practical purposes, since it is closely aligned to the question of sex. The main issue we must consider now is whether abortion is a Christian option. Should Christian conscience consent to the claim that abortion on simple demand is acceptable? Does the pregnant woman alone have the right to determine whether an abortion should be performed? To what extent may the Christian physician be a party to abortion proceedings?

The principles of the kingdom of God guide and govern God's people, whereas non-Christians have only the rules of the world to go by. For an unbeliever to abort a fetus, if the law permits, poses no moral problem. He is free to do so because it is legal. Indeed, the very presence of a law recognizing and sanctioning what he would like to do helps to allay any doubts in his mind.

According to Christian ethics, and indeed according to the law, a viable fetus must be delivered alive if possible. Certainly for the Christian no abortion should be performed except for extraordinary reasons, and the following would not apply: there can be no abortion for convenience or on simple demand, nor even in extraordinary circumstances unless the husband gives his consent. The Christian man and woman have become one flesh in Jesus Christ. For either wife or husband to make such a grave decision alone is contrary to the genius of the marriage relationship.

If the life of the mother is genuinely imperiled, then there is sufficient cause to abort. The reason is obvious: if the mother dies, the fetus perishes as well; it is better to save the life of the mother and lose the fetus than to witness the death of both. Of course this danger can be exaggerated, but the legitimate case should not be denied because of this possibility. Further, if there are compelling psychiatric reasons from a Christian point of view, mercy and prudence may favor a therapeutic abortion. If it can be demonstrated prior to quickening that a mongoloid child has been conceived, an abortion might appear to be permissible for the sake of the parents (although the writer knows of mongoloid children who have been a great blessing to Christian parents). However, this cannot be affirmed with certainty for the following reason: if the child at birth is a mongoloid, the same reasoning could be used to argue that it should be killed. And would not the acceptance of easy abortion logically lead to voluntary and involuntary euthanasia for the aged, and for many others, under the guise of social acceptability?

Although the world may approve of abortion for economic reasons or on the grounds that an unwanted child is unloved, the Christian cannot accept this view. He who believes that God cares for the birds of the field must believe also that God will care for his offspring; to talk of an unwanted child that cannot be loved is not in keeping with the Christian life style that accepts God's providence. Of course the presence of selfishness and egoistic unconcern is of the world and not of God, but we must not fail for this reason to take into account the love, the concern, and the providing and keeping power of God.

The 1973 decision of the Supreme Court of the United States, as written by Justice Blackmun, is illustrative of the present trend in American life. Disregarding Christian conviction which through the centuries has been opposed to abortion, the decision was that a woman has legal right of control over her body and, at least for the first six months of pregnancy, can obtain an abortion virtually on demand. While the court shied clear of the question of when fetal life becomes human, the decision itself specifically approved this hitherto heathen practice of pre-Christian days. Ironically, the Court overlooked the heathen Hippocratic Oath, which bound physicians not to abort a fetus.

Two other things were overlooked by the Court: the first is that no woman need get pregnant in any event. Since she has control over her body she can refrain from having sexual contacts. Second, and far worse, is the logical sequence to the Court's decision; for if a person has ultimate control over his or her body, then the person also has the right to commit suicide, a form of murder even though it does not involve another person. From the Christian standpoint no one has ultimate control over his or her body. Everyone bears in himself the image of God, and this means that God through revelation and through nature controls the physical life of every individual.

The decision of the Supreme Court stands on the side of paganism against Christianity. No justice who is a Christian can reconcile his decision with biblical Christianity.

No Christian should enter the marriage relationship unless he realizes that marriage has for its purpose more than the fulfillment of sexual needs, important as this is. For God also ordained marriage for the propagation of the human race. Therefore those who want marriage and sexual fulfillment have no excuse for not propagating the race simply because of the economic and other responsibilities which attend the rearing of children. Of course there are exceptional cases involving hemophilia, genetic abnormalities, etc., in which childless marriages would be quite legitimate.

The Christian physician and surgeon are confronted with a unique responsibility and an unusual opportunity concerning abortion. Under the principles of God's kingdom they can neither advocate nor participate in any unethical abortion. Outside of cases of rape, danger to the life of the mother, and perhaps gross retardation or mongoloidism, the Christian physician and surgeon are not free to use their skills for a purpose God disallows. Their right of conscience in the practice of medicine is inalienable; they must answer ultimately to God for their actions, not to men, medical societies, or the state. Thus Christian physicians and surgeons have an obligation to bear witness to their Christian convictions in the practice of medicine, and to refuse to perform or be an accessory to any abortion which is in defiance of the law of God. This will not, however, keep them from performing remedial medical services, if their skills are required subsequent to an abortion which they have not performed.

HOMOSEXUALITY

Any discussion of sex does not end with marriage, fornication, adultery, and abortion. Homosexuality, long regarded as an abnormality, has become prominent, and its apologists want everyone, even those who do not practice it, to regard it as a legitimate norm of life. The world now openly endorses homosexuality, and it increasingly surfaces through the theater, TV, and the news media. This is not surprising.

What is astonishing is the attempt by some Christians not only to condone homosexual behavior but to claim that it is fully in accord with Christian conduct, has the endorsement of the law of God, and is a legitimate channel for sexual fulfillment and love. Homosexuals (and lesbians) who claim to be Christians are vocal in defense of their different sexual practices. They argue that the Church becomes irrelevant and loses its capacity to minister by pronouncing judgment against homosexuality. Moreover, they loudly protest that their personhood is being attacked.

Loving concern for the homosexual and sympathy for his plight is one thing. Endorsing a practice that God severely condemns is another. Scripture clearly states that homosexuals are excluded from the kingdom of God (1 Cor. 6:9). Men cannot include what God excludes. God's revelation cannot be bent, even in sympathy, to support what God himself disallows. The question is not whether homosexuality is acceptable to the world, but whether it is a legitimate part of the life style of the new community in Jesus Christ. About this there can be no doubt. Old and New Testament Scriptures (Lev. 20:13; Rom. 1:27) alike pronounce judgment against the practicing homosexual, just as they pronounce judgment against drunkards, liars, and whoremongers, who also shall have no part in the kingdom of God.

Homosexual practices in private by consenting adults are not something the Church or the Christian can endorse. There is forgiveness, pardon, and hope for those who are ready to acknowledge their sin against God and repent. Paul says to the Corinthians, "Such were some of you." They have ceased from their homosexual behavior. But what of those who continue to have homosexual desires and remain Christian in profession? If they are unable to enter into a heterosexual relationship, they have no choice but to remain celibate. This may be difficult, but it is not impossible.

Many people do live without sex, legitimate or illegitimate. Sometimes invalidism of a marriage partner makes sex impossible. Does this justify promiscuity? No! Granted, homosexuals face a difficult choice. At stake is their destiny in God's kingdom; yet as God gives grace to those who forego sex for other reasons, so grace is available to homosexuals. They will surely experience temptation and have to endure hardship, for "narrow is the way that leads to eternal life." The homosexual road is the broad road that leads to destruction. Lack of will and conformity to the world, rather than inability to live in the Spirit, are what finally lead in that direction.

PORNOGRAPHY AND OBSCENITY

This section started with a discussion of the command not to commit adultery and then considered the command not to kill in relation to abortion. This in turn has to do with sex, as do adultery, fornication, and homosexuality. The discussion on sex also requires some consideration of pornography and obscenity.

Pornography is completely oriented toward sex. Its least erotic forms display the nude bodies of males and females. Until the advent of the camera, pornography depended on the skill of an artist who could draw pictures. However, the camera made possible the reproduction of the human figure in a way not possible for an artist to equal. The movie camera can do what the still camera is unable to do: produce multiplied numbers of "still" shots that are linked together sequentially and chronologically. Not merely one shot taken at an instant is available, but a continuous act of indefinite time length. In fact, the movie camera theoretically could make a pictorial record without interruption of the life of any individual from birth to death.

The advent of black and white and, later, color photography added a dimension that painters alone had enjoyed for centuries, and promptly opened still another door to this profitable industry based on man's known erotic nature. Almost without exception pornography preys upon people for financial gain, pandering to depraved appetites with the grossest and vilest displays. But pornographers also produce technically competent, sophisticated, low-key artistic productions that pass for art, and which are difficult for anyone to condemn without being charged with prudery and evil-mindedness.

Pornography, for the most part, is explicit, not simply suggestive. People who permit themselves to be photographed for pornographic purposes do so for a variety of reasons. Some simply have a depraved delight in exhibitionism. Some do it primarily for money. Many a Hollywood star has started her film career by this route. Marilyn Monroe furthered her career by allowing herself to be photographed in the nude. She was the favorite pin-up for thousands of soldiers after World War II.

Hard core pornography centers on the abnormal; it features homosexuals in action, as well as portrays the more common practices of adultery, seduction, and fornication. From there it proceeds to other things that decency forbids writing about.

Pornography involves more than visual aids of the *Playboy* type or those of cheaper and more disgusting forms. It includes the written page, whether in the artistic form of the novel, the biography, the autobiography, or various other genres. A picture, it has been said, is worth a thousand words, but the written word can enhance the erotic impact of pictures as well as stand on its own. Words can titillate even more strongly than pictures, for they can convey ideas and awaken the imagination in ways that pictures cannot. Words can describe the inner feelings, emotions, and thoughts of the characters depicted, and thus heighten the erotic response.

Pictorial and written pornography are powerful psychological and spiritual forces. They present their views of life in such a manner as to make the illicit appear desirable, moral, or at least normative. Pornographers do not warn their viewers and readers of the undesirable consequences stemming from their merchandise. Nor do the characters they describe often reap the harvest their actions deserve. They follow the pattern of liquor advertisers who picture men and women of distinction, not the debauched and sodden faces of drunkards as they lie senseless on the street or on the floor of the living room. Neither do they portray men and women in the grip of delirium tremens, or dead on the highways.

The pornographers don't paint word pictures or show films depicting the horrible death, stemming from paresis as a result of sexual misbehavior, of the Chicago gangster Al Capone. Nor do they speak of King Henry VIII, husband of six wives and seducer of many other women, whose death was occasioned at least in part by venereal disease. Adolf Hitler's twisted life can be accounted for, to a degree, by venereal disease. Nietzsche, the German "death-of-God" writer, spent the last ten years of his life in an insane asylum, brought about by sexual misconduct. Preserved in the ruins of Pompeii are pornographic paintings that may well explain the eruption of Mount Vesuvius as an act of divine judgment on that city. But anything found there is mild compared to the current crop of the pornographer's art.

Sweden and Denmark, where church attendance is at an all-time low, are the world capitals of pornography. It is difficult to imagine how it would be possible for anyone to exceed their attainments in this area.

The low state of Christianity may be explained in some

measure by the fact that Christians have been influenced and seduced mentally and morally, at a conscious and unconscious level, by this evil. Their standards of purity have been lowered; far too many Christians defend as good what former generations delineated as prurient, delighting in new-found freedom from the so-called prudery of earlier ages. Whereas in earlier times men may have failed to live up to their standards, in this era the standards themselves have diminished or altogether disappeared.

Christians should develop a new awareness of the blatancy, as well as the subtlety, of pornography. They should see more clearly that it is characteristic of the world; when they are sucked into the vortex of pornography they become worldly, their minds and hearts are defiled, their commitment to God is weakened, and their effectiveness as servants impaired.

Paul says Christians ought to think about whatever is pure and lovely (Phil. 4:8). As a corollary, whatever is impure and unlovely ought to be shunned. All pornography should be put away, and if there is any confusion over what constitutes pornographic material, the following criterion should be observed: whatever arouses erotic impulses, outside of those that belong properly and beautifully to marriage, should be regarded with suspicion and kept away from, in order to avoid the condemnation of God. The work of God is greatly hindered by carnal believers whose lives make the Cross of Jesus Christ of no effect. At a time in history when standards of conduct are at an all-time low, and when the barriers of holiness are being broken down by licentiousness, impurity, and sexual irregularities, Christians ought to rise to the challenge of living for God in such a way that the world will know they are true followers of Jesus Christ.

Pornography is opposed to the positive Christian virtue of modesty, which is regarded in the Bible as wholesome and desirable. Modesty has distinct cultural overtones, making it exceedingly difficult to set standards which would be applicable to every situation. Missionaries have made it all too plain that what the western world looks upon as modest or immodest varies considerably from non-Christian cultures. Today, however, the western world has lowered its standards in ways that would shock large segments of the non-western world. China, for example, has been characterized by Scotty Reston of the *New York Times* as puritanical in its morality.

Here a basic difference between male and female susceptibilities must be noticed. Men are more easily aroused by visual stimuli than women. It is rare for women to be attracted to men by their appearance alone; few women will be seen gazing at men along the street. But men will not only notice but may pursue more actively a woman whose immodest dress becomes a source of arousal.

Christian women do not always display an awareness of the effect their immodesty has on men. This is true on the street as well as on the beach and should not be overlooked. Both Paul and Peter speak plainly to the issue.

Paul says that "women should adorn themselves modestly and sensibly in seemly apparel" (1 Tim. 2:9). Peter argues for "reverent and chaste behavior . . . not the outward adorning with braiding of hair, decoration of gold, and wearing of robes, but let it be the hidden person of the heart with the imperishable jewel of a gentle and quiet spirit, which in God's sight is very precious" (1 Peter 3:2, 3). Both are saying that a certain modesty and circumspection in dress should characterize Christian women. Surely we should assume that anyone who has crucified the flesh with its passions and desires (Gal. 5:24) will avoid any mode of dress which is designed to draw undue attention to one's own person.

Modesty is God's answer to pornography. Where modesty reigns women will not permit themselves to become pawns for the merchants of sin whose livelihood depends on immodesty, which God abhors.

VIII. THINGS NOT PROHIBITED

Our discussion of worldliness as it pertains to conduct has dwelt on such express biblical commandments as "Thou shalt not steal, bear false witness, commit adultery, or kill." These are, for the most part, direct and easily comprehensible prohibitions. The Christian, however, is called upon to make decisions on many matters concerning which God has given no direct commandments. Such decisions cannot be made on the basis of principle but on the basis of expediency. Believers ought never do what is clearly unlawful. But some things ought not to be done even though they are not explicitly forbidden, falling into the category of acts that are inexpedient (1 Cor. 6:12; 10:23).

In his ministry to the church at Corinth the Apostle Paul dealt personally with a situation of this nature. The issue was whether it was permissible for Christians to eat meat that had been offered to idols and then placed on sale in the marketplace. As a result of some Christians buying and eating this kind of meat those less mature in the faith were hurt spiritually and were caused to stumble. Paul did not dodge the issue but examined the problem seriously. His conclusion was that idols have no real existence, therefore to eat meat offered to an idol is quite all right. There is no divine law against it. Then Paul asked a question as a guideline: may it still be wrong for a Christian to eat meat offered to an idol even when no commandment forbids it? His answer was "yes," and he laid down the rule of thumb that expediency must cover such occasions. Some things are lawful, he said, but not expedient. Because of love for the brethren one should refrain from a lawful thing if, in doing it, he causes a brother for whom Christ died to stumble. Paul concluded he would eat no meat offered to idols since it was not expedient even though lawful (1 Cor. 8:1 ff.).

ALCOHOL

Should Christians drink alcohol? Wine is surely not forbidden, although temperance is enjoined (1 Tim. 5:23; Prov. 20:1; Eph. 5:18; 1 Tim. 3:3; Prov. 23:21). Since total abstinence is not commanded here, the principle of expediency must take effect based on the current abuse of alcohol in modern society. First, we should consider that there are more than six million alcoholics in the United States and millions more on the verge of alcoholism. Second, drunken drivers are involved in at least half the accidents which kill approximately 150 Americans and injure another 11,000 on the highways every day. While a surgical resident at Massachusetts General Hospital in Boston, Dr. William C. Wood stated that approximately ninety per cent of the patients brought to his hospital for emergency treatment as a result of automobile accidents were either those who had been drinking or who had been hurt because of drunken driving by someone else. In 1972 the French National Institute for Health and Medical Research claimed that since 1949 deaths caused by alcoholism had risen eighty per cent for men and thirty-two per cent for women.

Third, alcohol is a depressant, and its immoderate use can

result in addiction and the lowering of moral barriers. Moreover, alcohol can do nothing of a medicinal nature that cannot be done better through proper medical attention. In this manner the unfortunate results that so often stem from its use can be avoided. If the chief value of alcohol lies in its power to produce a false conviviality, then the Christian surely does not need it.

In June of 1970, the *Reader's Digest* published an article entitled "Alcohol and Your Brain," by Albert Q. Maisel. In this article Maisel describes the effect alcohol has of depriving various layers of the brain of the oxygen essential for the functioning of the cells. This phenomenon is called sludging. Every drink destroys some of the brain cells irreplaceably; the heavier the drinker the greater the number of cells to die.

In addition, the professors at the Medical University of South Carolina have demonstrated that sludging can plug the capillaries of entire areas of an organ, and thus deprive the cells of the oxygen they so desperately need. Fewer and fewer cardiologists are prescribing alcohol to aid heart circulation because of mounting evidence that it may actually damage heart-muscle tissues.

On June 11, 1973, The *Washington Post* drew attention to the strong comeback alcohol is making among the young. More and more young people are consuming beer and wine. Recent studies in Michigan, where the legal drinking age was lowered from 21 to 18, show a 119 per cent increase in alcohol-related accidents involving the 18-20 age group. In Montgomery County, Maryland, the use of alcohol by senior high school students increased from 43.8 per cent in 1969 to 60.7 per cent in 1972. A nationwide survey by the National Commission on Marijuana and Drug Abuse reported that the use of alcohol by senior high school students increased 90 per cent between 1969 and 1972. Reports also indicate that alcoholism is becoming more widespread among pre-high school adolescents.

When one considers these statistics and ponders the numerous drawbacks to the use of alcohol, it remains for those who advocate its use to demonstrate its value and benefits. There is no argument in its favor that is not outweighed by the drawbacks. The Christian has a particular responsibility in this matter because of the significance his life style and influence have on others. In view of the facts, the case for abstinence now seems to go beyond the simpler question of expediency to the direct issue of principle. Since the body of the believer is the temple of the Holy Spirit, it is not difficult to conclude that abstinence is to be preferred even though there is no express prohibition in Scripture against the use of alcohol in moderation.

CIGARETTES

One habit long regarded by Christians as unclean and debilitating that now is held to be deleterious by the medical profession is the cigarette syndrome. Also in accordance with the conviction of many Christians is the daily mounting evidence that cigarette smoking is a positive factor in both lung cancer and cardio-vascular diseases. At first the report of the Surgeon General of United States made it necessary for cigarette manufacturers to state, "Warning, the Surgeon General has determined that cigarette smoking *may* be harmful to your health." Now the warning states "*is* dangerous to your health." In other words, "smoke at your own risk." If you buy what the manufacturer has warned is dangerous to your health, he is no longer liable for the consequences.

Dr. Ralph Byron, chief surgeon of the City of Hope cancer hospital in Duarte, California, has extensive data available to show that those who smoke two packs of cigarettes a day for twenty years are statistically far more likely to have lung tumors than those who don't. Women started smoking cigarettes later than men after advertising campaigns convinced them that it was not unladylike. Now the lung cancer statistics show that the incidence of this disease in women is following closely the pattern for men twenty years ago.

Thousands of people die every year from other diseases directly or indirectly attributable to cigarette smoking. Fully seventy-five per cent of the bed patients in hospitals today suffer from diseases related to cigarette consumption. These conditions finally got so bad in the United States that the government prohibited cigarette advertising on radio and TV, substituting instead flash warnings against smoking.

The conviction of many Christians over the years that cigarette smoking was harmful has now been thoroughly supported by the massive evidence gathered by morally neutral scientists. If the world is convinced of this evil, the Christian should not require further evidence. Inasmuch as the body of the believer is the temple of the Holy Spirit, nothing unclean or physically destructive should be allowed to enter it.

Recent reports claim that cigarette smoke is also dangerous when inhaled secondhand by non-smokers. Some of the rudest people are those smokers who thoughtlessly blow their smoke in the direction of non-smokers. There are numbers of Christians who do smoke, and the law of love would seem to warrant the opinion that the least they can do is refrain from doing so when among those who are not habituated and whose health may be affected by inhaling someone else's stale cigarette fumes.

From another perspective the Christian must take into account the addictive aspect of cigarettes. Many smokers are unable to break the habit once they become addicted. The Christian is to have control over his body, not his body over him. When he *must* have a cigarette, and when the absence of one produces uncomfortable reactions, he no longer controls his body. This is true whether the desire happens to be for cigarettes, food, sex, or anything else.

To a lesser degree what has been said about cigarettes may also be said about cigars and pipes. It is true, however, that the risk of lung cancer is reduced considerably if cigar and pipe users do not inhale the smoke; but the non-Christian may see little difference in any form of tobacco as it concerns the Christian's overt witness. The danger also remains, regardless of the form of tobacco, to the atmosphere, which is already dangerously polluted, and to the people who must breathe the air that has been contaminated by tobacco smoke.

DRUGS

What can be said about alcohol and tobacco can be said more cogently about drugs. This is the age of the pill—pain pills, sleeping pills, pep pills. No one can rightly question the use of drugs under adequate supervision of the medical fraternity. Drugs have enabled men to conquer some of the worst diseases and to bring healing and health to multiplied millions of people. But some drugs such as heroin, opium, and LSD have wrought havoc in the lives of many people. The drug traffic is one of the world's biggest businesses, built as it is on human weakness, and caters to a habit which, once formed, is extraordinarily difficult to break. When a person becomes addicted to hard drugs, the cost of the habit usually forces him into a life of crime to pay for it. Nothing can justify the use of hard drugs for the Christian or for anybody else.

Marijuana smoking is the current fad, the medical implications of which have by no means been fully developed and probably won't be for years to come. Some young people defend marijuana (pot) smoking by pointing out that their elders use alcohol and tobacco to excess, and rightly insist that alcoholism is the number one drug problem. At the same time they wonder why they should be criticized by those who smoke and drink heavily for using pot. But each habit must be examined on a separate basis and not casually thrown into some other category.

It is imprudent to play around with anything, the full effects of which are quite uncertain. A psychiatrist from the University of California at Berkeley has catalogued the ill effects of marijuana on the body, the mind, and the work habits of the user. The picture is a bleak one. Since it cannot be demonstrated that marijuana is neither toxic nor otherwise harmful, its value should be related to what useful purpose it may serve. Since there is no immediate or long range usefulness inherent in marijuana that cannot be found in other less baneful alternatives, no generally healthy individual needs the false support of that drug to live an exciting and fulfilling life. The Christian who has an all-out commitment to Christ will be so busy doing more positive things that he won't have time for a major habit-forming drug like heroin or a lesser one like marijuana.

It is difficult to decide whether marijuana should be made legal, particularly when society does not make alcohol and cigarettes illicit. We probably can never answer the question to the satisfaction of all as to where the line is to be drawn concerning those things which are declared illicit and those which are not. In Scripture, for example, drunkenness is condemned but drinking wine is not. Divorce is also condemned, but it was allowed because of the hardness of heart of the Israelites. But even if marijuana were to be legalized everywhere, this would not relieve the believer from shunning the habit and working by moral persuasion to convince others to abstain.

THEATER

For years attendance at the theater was frowned on by "spiritual" or "separated" Christians. However, the advent of TV has brought surprising changes. Movies made twenty and thirty years ago are now regular TV fare, and thousands of Christians, who never would have set foot in a theater, sit with eyes glued to the TV screen catching up on what they missed years before. As a result, the traditional fences barring Christians from the theater have come down and a new perspective prevails. Just about everyone agrees that in and of itself the motion picture is morally neutral. Like sex, the rightness or wrongness depends on how it is used and what its contextual relation is. Sex in marriage is beautiful and good; sex outside of marriage is not. The same act under one set of circumstances may be good; whereas under another set of circumstances it may be evil. So with the motion picture and the stage. For the Christian in his battle against the world the criterion for attending a film should be what is shown on the screen. Yet some Christians in good conscience may decide that the theater is not for them, even if the films are good. So be it for conscience's sake.

What is different today is the attitude adopted by many Christians toward stage productions and films that are bad. Under the guise of honesty, "telling it like it is," knowing what the world is all about, they argue that the Christian should be exposed to these things in order to be better equipped to meet the world on its own grounds. They do not feel that such contact will produce defilement and impair their holiness before the Lord. Now it may be true that to the pure all things are pure and nothing can defile them, but unfortunately no such person, other than Jesus Christ, has ever lived or ever will live in this world.

There can be little question about the propriety of watching good programs on TV and good films in the theater.

But what about the bad ones in the light of what has just been said? The flesh is weak and cannot be trusted. It is presumptuous to assume that one can look and not be influenced adversely. The insidious, cumulative effect of filth is such that a man can be overtaken and subverted without a conscious awareness of what is taking place. Moreover, it is thoroughly illogical to suppose that one cannot obtain knowledge apart from actual experience. One doesn't have to commit fornication or adultery to know what they are like, or get drunk to know about drunkenness; no one has to watch homosexuals and lesbians engage in their activities on the screen to understand such behavior or to be convinced that it is wrong. People do not drink poison in order to show that the chemical will kill those who drink it.

A good rule of thumb is to avoid what is questionable, to seek only those things which are good, and to slough off what cannot help but may harm one. The believer who is serious in his warfare against the temptations of the world ought not ask himself, "How far can I go?" but, "How close to Christ can I stay?" Therefore he should look at nothing and listen to nothing that will not promote spiritual growth, strengthen him in his faith and commitment, and keep him unspotted from the world. Sir Peter Lely, a rather well-known painter, made it a rule of his life never to dwell on a bad picture. The reason for this was that his mind would become obsessed by the bad painting to the point that his own work would become affected. He was not able to paint the best pictures when his mind and heart had been befouled by the bad.

DANCING

In the battle of the flesh, dancing has long been regarded as an alluring form of recreation and pleasure to be shunned by Christians who take seriously the teaching of Jesus that we are not of the world. It has generally been associated with the world, and in some instances has opened the door to fornication and adultery. Dancing brings erotic pleasure and excitation to the participants, although some men who dance ·allege that it has few or no erotic implications for them, while the erotic aspects seem to be even less formidable for women. In any discussion of the subject with young people one question inevitably surfaces. "Isn't it better for young people to dance in public under adequate supervision than for them to "make out" in parked cars?" The answer, of course, is "yes," if the question is genuinely an either/or. It *is* better to dance under chaperonage in a public place than to pet alone in lover's lane. But it may be better yet to do neither. Each activity must be gauged on the basis of its intrinsic value, not on the grounds that one is less or more sinful than another.

Dancing is a social activity, the acceptance or rejection of which is most frequently related to the cultural environment in which the individual moves. Every group with its own mores also has a cultural overhang. Among theological evangelicals there are sub-cultures characterized by some very specific taboos. Dancing is universally shunned among fundamentalists (a term used here in a sociological rather than a theological sense, for theologically there is little difference between the evangelical and the fundamentalist except that the latter is not infrequently a dispensationalist). Evangelicals, who are theologically fundamentalist, are often sociologically liberal. For them dancing may or may not be part of their cultural overhang. (We are not talking here about folk dancing or square dancing, which are quite innocuous. They are generally regarded as non-erotic in the same manner as ice skating and roller skating).

The principle of Christian liberty surely has some place in any discussion of dancing. The Scriptures do not specifically forbid it. David danced before the Lord (2 Sam.

6:14); Jesus, in the parable of the lost son, describes how there was music and dancing on the son's return to his father's house (Luke 15:25). Does not Christian liberty suggest that there are instances when, due to the traditions of certain cultures and sub-cultures, dancing may or may not be acceptable? A real and vexing problem is the attitude that develops on the part of those who abstain and thus judge those who do not as worldly. Contrariwise, many of those who dance have some very odd but definite opinions about people who do not.

I was raised in a sociological environment that saw no evil in dancing. Later I moved into a different sub-culture where dancing was taboo. I came to embrace the latter viewpoint but would not wish to legislate for others on this matter. Let Christian freedom prevail.

Nevertheless, in the midst of his freedom let every Christian remember that sex is an explosive and powerful force. It is so strong that there comes a point of no return, a point beyond which, once physiological stimuli have reached a peak, it is exceedingly difficult to stop or to reverse. In a sense, to play with sex is to play with fire. God has implanted the sex drive into the human race to guarantee the perpetuation of the species. How well this procreative force is being used may be seen from the population explosion of which we hear so much. How closely sex and dancing are associated may be seen in the fact that men normally will not dance together, nor is there any enjoyment in it for them if they do. However, let each one decide for himself in the light of the facts.

The sharp disjunction between the Christian and the world has been losing its edge in America in recent decades. There have been vast social changes which in some instances have been for the good. Any teaching on separation is more apt to verge on legalism than it is to fall into the pit of antinomianism. I recall one missionary who distributed to the members of a home church an instruction sheet concerning social taboos in the country to which he was going as a missionary. He was enjoined never to wear a bow tie, not to cross his legs in church, and, when in the pulpit, not to put his hand in his pocket. Lipstick, as well as certain kinds of clothing, was forbidden for his wife. These prohibitions would be laughable if they were not real. But the point for us to remember is that we must distinguish between the prohibitions of God and those of men. God's prohibitions do not have for their end the taking away of anything good from his people. No Christian should equate his own cultural prohibitions with those expressly commanded by God. And if he remembers that man-made rules are finite and may often depend on the cultural climate of a sub-group, he will be less judgmental, more lenient of those who disagree with him, and always willing to let love cover a multitude of differences.

CARD PLAYING

Playing cards have been associated with gambling, fortunetelling, conjuring, and divination for hundreds of years. For this reason, they have long been frowned on by many Christians. The Puritans called them "the devil's picture book," and they and many other Protestants thought it sinful even to have a deck of cards in the house. Until the twentieth century playing cards were used mainly for gambling purposes; but with the advent of contract Bridge, invented by Harold Vanderbilt in 1921, the situation changed.

The idea of card games has not been regarded by Christians as evil *per se*. Rook was developed in the nineteenth century and has been played widely by people opposed to gambling. Rook has been called missionary Bridge, and even so noted an evangelist as Charles E. Fuller was an avid Rook fan.

How playing cards got their start and who gave them their form (e.g., jack, queen, king, ace) is not known precisely. Although playing cards have long been associated with gambling, we have seen that the situation can change. Other cultural customs long regarded as sinful or at least questionable have also yielded to changing times and have become acceptable.

A good illustration of this has to do with cosmetics. Christian women formerly did not use lipstick, nail polish, or eyebrow paint. These were left to prostitutes. In 1770 a bill was introduced into the English Parliament with the following provisions:

> That all women of whatever age, rank, profession, or degree, whether virgins, maids, or widows, that shall, from and after such Act, impose upon, seduce, and betray into matrimony, any of His Majesty's subjects, by the scents, paints, cosmetic washes, artificial teeth, false hair, Spanish wool, iron stays, hoops, high heeled shoes, bolstered hips, shall incur the penalty of the law in force against witchcraft, and like misdemeanors and that the marriage, upon conviction, shall stand null and void.

Humorous as this may appear to moderns of our day, Colonial America also had at least one interesting view concerning cosmetics. New England was Puritan and the South was liberal, but even Quaker Pennsylvania, which occupied middle ground between them, had on the statute books the notorious Act of 1770 "by virtue of which a marriage might be annulled if it could be proved that the wife had, in courtship, deceived and misled her husband by using cosmetics."

Perhaps we can clear away the smog surrounding the use

of playing cards by several observations. First, it is as easy
to gamble with Rook cards as with playing cards, just as it
is to gamble with dice used in playing Monopoly; but it
need not be so. Contract Bridge is a twentieth century
game and there is nothing intrinsically wrong or offensive
in it. People may (but many don't) gamble at Bridge;
people can (and some do) gamble with Rook cards. Therefore the gambling argument against the use of cards is not
persuasive. Second, it would appear that playing Bridge is
not wrong in principle. If playing Bridge is not wrong in
principle, then the question must be settled on the basis of
deciding whether the game is worth the time involved. Let
no man's conscience be bound; let each decide for himself,
taking into account any possible offense he might give or
stumbling block that he might become. And let him who
refrains not sit in judgment on his brother who doesn't.

GAMBLING

Any discussion of card playing raises the question of
gambling, which must be considered in a larger perspective.

Dr. David L. McKenna, the president of Seattle Pacific
College, served as chairman of the Governor's *Ad Hoc*
Committee on Gambling for the State of Washington. He
wrote an article on gambling, published in the June 8, 1973,
issue of *Christianity Today*. In it he spoke of three forms
of gambling: social, professional, and governmental.

Social gambling includes private games of chance (for
example, poker played in someone's living room). The play-
ers remain on equal terms. This form of gambling is looked
upon as an individual's privilege and has been extended,
usually for religious or charitable purposes, to include bingo
and raffles. Church bingo, McKenna said, is "the trunk upon
which a tree of gambling was built."

Professional gambling, whether in Las Vegas or Timbuktu,

usually is conducted in a licensed gaming parlor. It is big business and goes from slot machines to card games to dice to roulette, etc. In professional gambling there is always a "house cut." For example, slot machines are regulated so that for every dollar spent the house will keep from twenty to forty cents. The person who plays it once and hits the jackpot will win if he plays no more. But whoever plays the slot machines consistently will end up poorer. McKenna stated in his article that his committee was told by an assistant attorney general that "the possibility of cheating in gambling is limited only by the human imagination."

Government gambling is the third form, consisting generally in state lotteries and pari-mutuels. The rationale for lotteries, which seem to be increasingly popular, is that they produce tax revenues in a more painless fashion at a time when people are psychologically set for a "tax rebellion." But when lotteries peter out, the states must then adopt the market mentality in order to encourage people to buy lottery tickets.

Wherever there is legalized gambling, organized crime enters the picture; and even if organized crime were not involved, unregenerate human nature is such that all sorts of subterfuge, cheating, and other illegalities would accompany the practice nevertheless.

Now it is true that Scripture does not specifically prohibit gambling. But it is obviously a vice that runs counter to the biblical principle of stewardship. It encourages the notion that chance determines all results; this goes against the biblical teaching that God, not chance, governs the affairs of men and of nations.

Certainly social gambling cannot be prevented, but the Christian should at least work for laws that will prevent cheating and corruption. Professional gambling, which is always accompanied by violence, prostitution, and drug abuse, should be opposed vigorously by Christians and prevented wherever possible from being legalized. State lotteries are a poor substitute for direct taxation, hiding as they do the true situation from the taxpayer. But gambling is a corrupting habit that despoils public life, hurts those who engage in it, and can lead to crime.

For the Christian the facts connected with gambling make it so obviously inconsistent with the biblical life style, the Christian ethic, and the principles of expediency, that it should be shunned like the plague.

One further word should be added by way of a footnote. There are a number of Christian institutions whose parietal rules explicitly forbid among other things, playing cards and gambling. Whoever joins himself to such an institution, whether as a student or a faculty member, falls within the ground rules and voluntarily submits himself to them. In such a fraternal relationship he is honor bound to abide by the agreement, and he is less than a gentleman if he makes an issue of or undercuts that to which he has bound himself by free choice. No situation will be totally free of ambiguities, and rarely will any set of parietal rules be equally satisfactory to everyone.

In the nature of things, external, visible activities easily take precedence in the minds of many people over more important but less visible ones. Thus the emphasis on smoking, dancing, etc. But are not anger, gossip, backbiting, and an unloving spirit more formidable ones than the others we have dealt with? Of course they are. It is less easy to face them honestly, but the failure to do so should be a matter of great concern. While we should not weigh one fault against another, it is quite possible that the Christian who smokes can approximate the ideals of love and forbearance more than one who doesn't smoke cigarettes but does gossip, tell tales, and manifest anger and an unforgiving spirit. It would be a grave error to concentrate on certain outward physical habits and leave untouched those spiritual delinquencies that are even more weighty.

The true hallmark of the Christian life is love—love of God and of one's fellow man. Love covers a multitude of sins; it is less judgmental and more compassionate. Love puts up with what non-love would never tolerate, bears the other fellow's burden, is kind as well as longsuffering. If we must disagree about some of these matters let it be done in love, allowing the ones with whom there is disagreement that liberty which is rightfully theirs in Christ to make their decisions under the guidance of the Holy Spirit. Let us not set up for any man rules that cannot be firmly supported in Scripture, and in other matters allow for liberty, that we neither overburden some nor put a stumbling block in the path of others.

IX. THE CHRISTIAN AND SOCIETY

Two hundred years ago large segments of the earth were either uninhabited or sparsely populated. Today the situation has changed radically. With the exception of portions of Australia or regions of the planet that definitely are not habitable, the remainder of the land has become densely populated and is getting more so each year. The enlarging population has coalesced into political and social units in which groups rather than individuals have become important. Consequently, individual freedom has been curtailed in the interest of the group.

For example, a small family living in an isolated wilderness can do pretty much as it pleases. It is not concerned with its neighbors and its activities have little influence on others. But when people gather together in a community, almost immediately restrictions on individual freedom are imposed. Traffic lights go up, speed limits are set, sanitary provisions are legislated, and even noise levels are established.

The ethical life of the Christian in society takes on two dimensions: one has to do with his personal or private ethics, the other with social or community ethics. Sometimes there is a distinct overlap between personal and social ethics; sometimes there is little relation between them.

What the thought life of the Christian centers on is his personal business; no community can legislate successfully in this area. What the Christian thinks is his own private and personal affair. At this level he is responsible only to himself and to God. But when he seeks to translate his personal thoughts into outward actions, it usually becomes a community matter. A man can be an anarchist in his thought life, but when he commences to bomb buildings and kill, it is no longer a personal matter. It belongs to the community.

In the Old Testament God laid down regulations for community life. However, when the Jews were dispersed among the nations after A.D. 70, they, and the Christians after Pentecost, lived among peoples whose social ethics were pagan rather than Judeo-Christian.

Today there are no Christian nations per se. Rather, there are groups of Christians living in nations whose social laws have been influenced by the Judeo-Christian tradition, but there is no state whose standards of life are distinctively Christian. Nor is there any likelihood that there will ever be a purely Christian nation. States, in the main, have always been secular, not Christian.

In secular states Christians have to accept laws and customs with which they are not in agreement. In the United States, as elsewhere, pornography is rampant. Freedom of speech has become virtually absolute. Abortion on demand exists in practice if not wholly in principle. Gambling is legal. Prostitution goes unchecked. The drug traffic increases daily.

In this situation the Christian is faced with some hard choices. Knowing that prostitution will continue and laws prohibiting it will be breached, he may conclude that the interests of society will be furthered if it is legalized and placed under strict government and medical controls. If he thinks this, does it mean he implicitly approves of prostitution?

Gambling provides a similar problem. It has largely been controlled by mobsters who have made large fortunes from it, and will continue, legally or illegally, whether the Christian likes it or not. Is it not better, then, to legalize gambling and place it under government supervision?

The traffic in drugs is a persistent and increasing problem. Despite government efforts the illegal flow of narcotics into the United States has not been halted. Once an individual becomes addicted a life of crime to support the habit usually follows. Many robberies have for their sole purpose the securing of money to purchase narcotics. Would it not be better for society to provide free narcotics, or narcotics at a very low cost, so that addicts would not have to steal money to pay for drugs? For once the profit motive in the sale of drugs is removed, the pushers, the international gangsters, and the criminals are out of business. Such is the problem the Christian faces and to which he must respond.

The Christian, in situations such as these, has three alternatives. On the one hand he can opt out and do nothing, simply refusing to dirty his hands with something he doesn't like. But has the Christian discharged his obligations to God, government, and society by opting out? Is not benign neglect or disengagement at this point a decision in favor of the very thing the Christian professes against?

The second alternative is to stand firmly and unequivocally against those things Christian conscience cannot accept. This means that the believer must work for legislation that will make his viewpoint the law of the land, and also work to secure the most rigid enforcement of the law by the police power of the state.

The third alternative is to accept the fact that no state can become thoroughly Christian at all points. Thus the Christian acknowledges that there will be things unbelievers do that he himself would not do, but which would not be illegal so far as the state is concerned. However, it works out that the actions of the individual inevitably have social repercussions requiring specific limitations. In a sinful society the Christian may well have to settle for half a loaf rather than a whole one. But he needs uncommon good sense to know what to oppose in principle and what to accept with express limitations and restrictions.

The use of alcohol is a case in point. It is hardly likely that prohibition will ever prevail again in American society. But public drunkenness, driving an automobile while under the influence of alcohol, and the sale of alcohol to minors should be restricted by society, whether Christian or not.

A particularly difficult situation faces the Christian concerning homosexual activity. Although it is condemned by God, there is little that the state can do about what individuals do in the privacy of their bedrooms. This raises the question of whether the state has a right to tell citizens what they can or cannot do in private. What a person does in public is quite different from what he does in private. And who he does it with makes a big difference. The very least the Christian must stand for concerning homosexual activity is that it be confined to consenting adults in private. But any overt public act or solicitation, and any homosexual advances to minors, should be treated with severe penalties.

There are no easy guides for the Christian on how he ought to respond to questions of a social nature. As never before, there is a need for evangelicals to forge a common viewpoint on complex and difficult matters which are important to community life and the maintenance of an orderly society. One thing is clear, however. No Christian need do anything just because there is no law against it. No Christian woman need have an abortion because the law permits it. No Christian need gamble because it is legal. No believer need get drunk in his home because there is no law against it. All of this leads us to a consideration of certain subjects, both personal and social in nature, which concern the larger community.

MARRIAGE AND DIVORCE

Marriage is the tie that holds the family and society together. In virtually every society, Christian and non-Christian alike, marriage is an important social phenomenon. There are important differences, to be sure, but the institution itself is secure. In some parts of the world polygamy is common and divorce rare. In Mohammedan lands, for example, a man can have four wives at one time, and divorce is very simple. In the Western world monogamy is the norm, but easy divorce laws can turn it into a special form of polygamy. What does the Bible have to say about marriage and divorce in the overall plan of God for mankind?

The great teaching of the Bible is that the man and woman joined in marriage become one flesh. Paul says, "For this reason a man shall leave his father and mother and be joined to his wife, and the two shall become one" (Eph. 5:31). Elsewhere Paul states that the sexual act, even when performed with a harlot, makes the partners of this illicit relationship one body. "Do you not know," he says, "that he who joins himself to a prostitute becomes one body with her?" (1 Cor. 6:16).

In Ephesians Paul speaks of marriage and the union of the sexes as a mystery which is analogous to Christ and his bride the church (Eph. 5:32). In the Old Testament God saw that it was not good for man to be alone. Thus Eve was created out of Adam's rib as a fit helper to walk by his side (Gen. 2:18 ff.). In the Garden of Eden marriage was perfect. One of the results of Adam's fall, however, was the alienation that came between man and woman, between husband and wife. This should not be surprising when we consider the alienation which has taken place in all of life and in every human relationship since that time.

The man was made head over the woman (1 Cor. 11:3; Eph. 5:23). In the ideal state the headship of the man could cause no problem because of the perfection of the marriage relationship. But in a sinful world the headship of the man is a problem. It used to be part of the marriage ceremony that the woman promised to obey her husband, and he promised to love his wife but not to obey her. This stipulation is now eliminated from most modern ceremonies, although it hardly changes the Pauline teaching for the Christian. Indeed, that teaching is very strong. "Wives, be subject to your husbands, as to the Lord . . . As the church is subject to Christ, so let wives be subject in everything to their husbands" (Eph. 5:22, 24).

In every relationship there is need for a final authority in decision making. The parents were intended by God to make the final decisions concerning the family. Children are enjoined to obey their parents, which is an order for non-Christians just as it is for Christians (Eph. 6:1). God's creation ordinance granting Adam headship over his wife was based on the fact that he was created first. But this gave him no liberty to demand of his wife what is inconsonant with God's revelation.

Supposedly, a Christian couple will make corporate decisions satisfactory to both partners. This necessarily involves dialogue, give and take, and a willingness on the part of both to make concessions. After all, neither husband nor wife is always going to come to the right decisions. But who is to make the final decision when husband and wife are not in agreement? In such cases someone has to make the decision, and God has granted this responsibility to the man. Yet women are in no sense inferior to men, and not infrequently the judgment of the wife may be better than that of her husband. Hopefully, the husband in such an event will defer to the opinion of his wife. If he does not and the wife remains adamant, the marriage is in trouble. The stubborn wife, when faced with an opinionated and stubborn husband, can give in to him or, if she wants to, leave him. But is this Christian?

Marriage was intended by God to be elevating, wholesome, fulfilling, and happy. It was also intended to be permanent and indissoluble. The marriage mandate was laid down before Adam and Eve had any children and before there were any parents. "Therefore a man leaves his father and mother and cleaves to his wife, and they become one flesh" (Gen. 2:24). The doctrine of one flesh negates the idea of divorce. Christian marriage ceremonies all reflect this teaching, and the parties to the marriage covenant before God to stay together until death parts them.

Under the old covenant Israelite society was marred by much divorce and remarriage. Divorce was contrary to the will of God, yet Moses was allowed to set up a law governing its occurrence. The husband had to give his wife a bill of divorcement, which meant that he surrendered his claim on her dowry. Moses further stipulated that if she became another man's wife (which was permissible under the Mosaic law) she could not remarry her former husband in case she were divorced a second time or became a widow.

Jesus was asked by the Pharisees whether it was lawful for a man to divorce his wife for any cause. He noted the old covenant arrangements for divorce and answered: "What therefore God has joined together, let no man put asunder" (Mt. 19:6). As soon as he said this the Pharisees jumped at the opportunity to pit Jesus against Moses, the great lawgiver. For anyone to take exception to the teaching of Moses was unheard of. So they asked him, "Why then did Moses command one to give a certificate of divorce, and to put her away?" (Mt. 19:7). Jesus replied, "For your hardness of heart Moses allowed you to divorce your wives, but from the beginning it was not so." Then Jesus laid down his own dictum, which enlarged the law of Moses. He said, "Whoever divorces his wife, except for unchastity, and marries another, commits adultery" (Mt. 19:9).

There are two important details here in the teaching of Jesus. The first concerns adultery in relation to the law of Moses. Under the old covenant, if anyone committed adultery there was no need for a divorce, for the guilty parties were stoned to death, leaving the innocent spouse free to remarry. Under the new covenant, however, adulterers were not stoned to death, but the injured or innocent party nevertheless was entitled to a divorce and was free to remarry. However, in this context Jesus is dealing more with divorce unrelated to adultery. His teaching here is plain: divorce is wrong. But men are sinners, and so the law of Moses made a concession to human weakness and allowed for divorce. Jesus goes on to say, in contrast to the Mosaic law, that the divorced person (apart from adultery) who remarries is then guilty of adultery.

Regrettably, marriage does not turn out well for every Christian. We are not here talking about the unfortunate consequences that often occur when a believer and an unbeliever are married, for the Christian is specifically enjoined not to marry an unbeliever (2 Cor. 6:14 ff.). The believer who does so has no one to blame but himself or herself, if such a marriage does not work. But even marriages of believers do not always work. What is the Christian to do if his or her marriage is an utter failure?

Paul deals with the issue of divorce for the Christian and says his teaching is from God. Husbands are not to divorce their wives and wives ought not to leave their husbands. But if they do leave, they either must remain single or be reconciled to their husbands (1 Cor. 7:10 ff.). Apparently Paul is saying that people do not have to live together if the situation becomes impossible. But he is also saying that separation is one thing, divorce another. To be separated means to remain married but to live apart; to remarry while separated means to commit bigamy. Divorce always carries with it the assumption that possible remarriage is in the offing. Paul forbids remarriage, and Jesus states that whoever marries a divorced person commits adultery.

There is no way of getting around the teaching of Paul and of Jesus that remarriage following divorce, except for adultery, is forbidden. It is not difficut to see how rationalization can take over with each of two divorced people waiting for the other to remarry first, thus committing adultery and setting the other party free to remarry without guilt. Does remarriage of the Christian which does involve committing adultery mean that the continuance of the relationship is persistent adultery, or does the first act of sexual intercourse end the adultery?

The remarried Christian does place himself in an ambiguous situation. Obviously divorce does not end the natural desire for sexual fulfillment. Thus divorced persons are often caught between sinning if they remarry and burning with lust if they don't. Divorce is no more or less forbidden than lying, cheating, and stealing; but Christian charity may suggest remarriage as the lesser of two evils if there is extreme sexual desire accompanied by acknowledgement of the sin of divorce with sincere repentance, remorse, and the intention of obeying the law of God on marriage in the future. But this surely would not hold for the twice or thrice divorced person who professes Christian faith.

Plainly, from the standpoint of Christian social ethics, the state should regulate divorce but not forbid it. This is a matter that properly belongs to the conscience of the individual for it is predominantly a religious question concerning which the Christian ought not to bind the consciences of unbelievers.

RACISM

One of the greatest of all social curses is racism. In America this is thought of primarily as white racism directed against the Negro. That there is white racism, and that racism is a sin from the Christian perspective, cannot be denied. Racism, however, is not limited to relations between blacks and whites, but takes numerous forms.

For example, there is a great deal of black racism in Africa, directed in part against Asians. Great Britain was forced to admit thousands of Asians who were ordered by the government to leave Uganda, and whose wealth and properties were confiscated in the process. However this may be disguised, it was nothing less than naked racism.

There is also black racism directed against blacks. In Burundi tens of thousands of Negroes have been slain by other Negroes, an illustration of racism based not on skin color but on ethnic differences.

In India there is racial hatred for the Nagas, a tribal people under the domination of the Indian government. The Indians and the Pakistanis cordially detest one another, in still another aspect of racism. In Europe, the Germans and the Russians have hated one another through the centuries.

Racism can take religious forms as well. Catholics and Protestants in Northern Ireland hate one another with a vengeance. On the island of Cyprus, Muslims and Greek Orthodox have no use for one another.

Racism can also be in the form of nationalism, people of one nation hating those of another. The Egyptians and the Israelis are a case in point. The Czechs and the Hungarians hate the Soviet Union, their oppressor. The Irish hate the British. There is no end to the varieties of national racism.

Sometimes racism is based on supposed genetic differences. Some people argue that for someone to marry a member of another race is to mongrelize his own. Is there any truth in this claim? For those who take the Bible data seriously, racism cannot be sustained. Adam and Eve were the first human pair; all humanity has descended from them. The fall of Adam affected him and the whole race of men. If all men come from the same common ancestor, racism has no biological basis.

There is nothing in nature or in the Bible prohibiting intermarriage. It should be recalled that there are some Indians as dark-skinned as Africans but who are in fact Caucasians. The Ethiopians are as dark as Negroes but are not considered Negroid. Whatever the skin color, there is nothing wrong in principle for a person of one race to marry someone of another race. It may be inexpedient to do so for a variety of reasons, but this is a matter of personal choice.

Racism in any form is a denial of the law of love, for Christians are commanded to love their neighbors as they love themselves. On this basis, at least for the Christian, it is impossible either to justify or excuse racism. Unfortunately, human experience gives us no reason to hope for the elimination of racism; it will always be with us in one form or another. Nevertheless, for a Christian to be a racist means spiritual defeat and indicates a worldly frame of mind.

The Christian may have difficulty loving people of another national origin or skin color. This involves transitory subjective feelings and emotional attitudes. But even when love comes hard, the Christian can at least act justly toward others seeing that all people have equality under the law. In the United States many black people are asking for justice, not for intermingling of blacks and whites. Justice includes equal opportunity and the absence of discrimination in economic, political, educational, and other spheres. There are many areas in which prejudice and discrimination have been broken down through legislation of statutes by the courts and their enforcement by the police. There was a time when Negroes were segregated in trains, buses, and eating establishments. Today such discrimination has ceased. And it is apparent that legislation has worked successfully.

Evangelicals have stressed the need for changing the hearts of men in order to change their conduct. This idea is correct but its power is circumscribed by one unconquerable problem: even if all Christians acted as Christians ought to act, racism would not disappear, for vast numbers of people would still remain unregenerated. Therefore, the only way this situation can be handled is to require men by law to act justly whatever their feelings or attitudes may be. There is a sense, then, in which justice can and must be legislated, especially for those whose hearts are not right towards God.

It never is, and never will be, easy to determine how far one can go in this area without impinging on human freedom and the rights of the individual. Surely a Christian should be free to own a business and employ only Christians. But at what point does the number of employees remove the business from a purely private status to that embracing public interest? Evangelicals have a long way to go in working their way through to a Christian life and world view that takes all these things into account.

ANTI-SEMITISM

Anti-Semitism is a form of racism, but owing to its unique nature it is worthy of special consideration. It is a worldwide phenomenon consisting in hatred of the Jews. Many professing Christians in the past have been, and many are today, anti-Semitic. The Roman Catholic Church across the centuries has exhibited anti-Semitism, as well as have various other churches. What lies at the root of this evil?

Anti-Semitism, in part, is the judgment of God himself upon his chosen people because of their apostasy. Occupying a special place in God's plan of the ages, the Jews had a great responsibility. To them was given the revelation of God, the Old Testament Scriptures. They were the custodians of God's revelation, maintaining its purity. Through the Levitical sacrifices man could approach God by faith and receive the gift of justification and the forgiveness of sins. Through them also came the Messiah.

God promised his people blessings for faithfulness and curses for disobedience. Because they chose the latter, the wrath of God fell on them. The Scripture was fulfilled which said: " . . . the Lord will scatter you among all peoples, from one end of the earth to the other; and there you shall serve other gods, of wood and stone. . . . And among these nations you shall find no ease, and there shall be no rest for the sole of your foot; but the Lord will give you there a trembling heart, and failing eyes, and a languishing soul; your life shall hang in doubt before you" (Deut. 28:64-66).

The fact that persecution of the Jews is a result of the judgment of God in no way excuses those who treat the Jews this way. The persecutors do not act righteously even though they are unknowingly executing God's judgment. They shall some day give an account of their conduct.

Some Christians have felt justified in mistreating the Jews because of what they did to Jesus Christ, and many have gone so far as to label them "Christ-killers." Now it is a historical fact, despite the spate of claims denying it, that the Jews were responsible for the death of Christ (Acts 2:23, 36; 4:10). But while the Jews were the immediate agents in Jesus' crucifixion, the Gentiles were equally guilty of his death. To single out the Jews and make them the scapegoats is hardly biblical, for Jew and Gentile alike crucified the Lord of Glory.

In another sense it is rather far-fetched to blame the Jews of today for killing Jesus. God requires that every man give account of himself. The Mosaic law specified: "The fathers shall not be put to death for the children, nor shall the children be put to death for the fathers; every man shall be put to death for his own sin" (Deut. 24:16). It is wrong indeed to hold against the Jews of our day the sin their fathers committed in crucifying Jesus.

There are more Jews in the United States than in any other country in the world. They are sensitive to anti-Semitism and fight it tooth and nail. Sometimes they think there is anti-Semitism where it is non-existent. What really angers the Jews, however, are the efforts to proselytize them to the Christian faith. This has produced great tensions.

Christians hold tenaciously to the belief in freedom of religion, which includes the right to convert from one religion to another as well as the right to propagate one's religion freely through non-intimidating means of persuasion. Of course this is a two-way street, for Jews have just as much right as Christians to secure converts. This means they can witness to Christians about Judaism. We must honestly use the term "proselytism," but in the true sense of what it means. To persuade anyone to become a Christian is proselytism. The Christian can never be truly Christian and rule this out. This is the Christian's business because heaven and hell are the choices that demand a response.

The Jews today seem to suggest that proselytism itself is a form of anti-Semitism. Moreover, they resent the implicit idea that Judaism in itself is not sufficient. The Christian does not believe that witnessing to Jews and persuading them to become Christians is anti-Semitism. This is a red herring, but if it is true that evangelizing the Jew is really anti-Semitism (which Christians do not think it is), then the Christian has no choice but to continue his witnessing to Jews. He is commanded by God to do this, and disobedience would be a denial of God's authority. At the same time, the Christian boldly states that all men, Jew and Gentile alike, are lost if they do not receive Christ as their Savior. Thus Judaism without Christ is not sufficient. Christ is the fulfillment of Judaism, and a Jewish Christian is a fulfilled Jew. Indeed the New Testament clearly teaches that the Gentiles who confess Jesus as Lord are grafted into the stock of Israel and become by faith the children of Abraham (Rom. 9-11).

Billy Graham has spoken plainly against "gimmicks, coercion, and intimidation" in evangelizing Jews or anybody else. He has said: "In my evangelistic efforts I have never felt called to single out the Jews as Jews nor to single out any other particular groups, cultural, ethnic, or religious." He was saying that he preaches the Gospel to all men alike who do not know Jesus Christ as Savior.

No Christian who is walking in the Spirit can be anti-Semitic. Anti-Semitism violates the express commandment of God, the teaching of the apostle Paul, and the law of love. Jesus was a Jew. Virtually all of the New Testament was written by Jews. Christianity had its origin in Judaism. Every true believer accepts the Old Testament scriptures of the Jews to be the Word of God just as much as in every sense the New Testament is. The Christian must love the Jews and be grateful for what Judaism has brought to him in Jesus, the Jewish Messiah.

THE CHRISTIAN AND MARXISM

Communism (and also Marxism) is a twentieth century phenomenon that has enjoyed great success. Controlling a large segment of the world's population, it has even penetrated the Church of Jesus Christ; for there are numbers of professing Christians who are also Marxists. As a result there is no escaping the question of whether it is possible for a Christian to be a Marxist.

The only way the question can be answered intelligently is to examine the basic premises of Christianity and Communism to see whether they agree or conflict with one another. If they are antithetical then one cannot be both and remain consistent. In such a case the Communist would have to throw out Christianity and the Christian repudiate Marxism. It is true that Communism regards Christianity as an opiate of the people. Wherever Communism has come into political power it has muzzled the Christian churches, persecuted Christians, and engaged in overt police action and education campaigns to stamp out religion, Christian or otherwise. Stated another way, Communism recognizes religion as its greatest enemy, therefore it must fight religion if it is to survive.

Communism is anti-religious and a foe of Christianity; how then can it be possible for a Christian to be a Communist, if a Communist cannot be a Christian? In some instances those who simultaneously profess Christianity and Marxism are simply unbelievers, tares among the wheat. Some of them are true but ignorant believers, not realizing that they hold opposing and irreconcilable viewpoints. Some of them simply have warm hearts and soft heads.

What attracts some Christians to Marxism are the obvious economic inequalities around the world that Marxism promises to end. In Latin America, for example, fewer than 10% of the people own 90% of the land. Great wealth exists side by side with great poverty. Masses of people suffer from social injustice with little hope of any substantial change. The people with the great wealth perpetuate the status quo and do little or nothing to improve the temporal conditions of the masses. Then along comes Communism with its promises to create a brave new world in which there will be full equality, adequate material benefits for all, and complete social justice. Communism promises to cure the world's ills and establish a paradise on earth.

The Christian naturally identifies with an ideology that is interested in social justice, material benefits, and a Utopian world. Communism presents a compelling dream, even to Christians, because they and so many others literally have everything to gain (or so it appears) and nothing to lose, except their poverty and social injustice. For multitudes any change would be an improvement, or so they think. What they do not know is that there is a great difference between what Communists claim Communism to be and what it actually is. They also do not realize that there is a great gap between Communist promises and Communist performance. Nor are they able to detect the difference between propaganda and fact.

What is there about Communism that marks it off as un-Christian and makes it antithetical to biblical faith?

First of all, Communism is materialistic in its explanation of the origin of the universe and of man. It regards matter, not spirit, as eternal. Materialism is necessarily atheistic and non-personal. By contrast, Christianity starts with spirit and a person; thus the first principles of Christianity and Communism are opposites.

Secondly, at the heart of the Communist system is the dialectical principle of thesis, antithesis, and synthesis. The existing situation, thesis, is challenged by its opposite, the antithesis. In the ensuing conflict the thesis and antithesis are united in a synthesis. This in turn becomes the new thesis, which is followed by its antithesis leading to another synthesis. This occurs until Communism at last emerges and ushers in utopia. Man therefore becomes perfect and no longer needs the state which has withered away. The economic principle is: "To each according to his need; from each according to his ability."

However, until utopia comes socialism is the intermediate stage, consisting of state capitalism in which the means of production are owned by the state (meaning the people, or the proletariat). In the Soviet Union there are about 12 million members of the Communist Party, a small minority controlling the great majority. This is hardly a dictatorship of the proletariat, when most of the proletariat cannot become card-carrying Party members.

Democracy in Communist lands is a one-party system. There can be only one right party, for the presence of other parties would constitute bourgeois error. The people go to the polls to vote for one candidate for each job, with each one being assured of virtually a 100% stamp of approval. A one-party democracy is hardly a democracy in which freedom of choice can be exercised.

Communism is opposed to the profit motive, arguing that the capitalist extorts from the laborer the just fruits of his labor. This belief is based on the notion that the difference in value between the raw material and the finished product is due solely to labor. When the laborer does not get this full return he is being cheated. The profit is what the capitalist, the non-producer, takes illegitimately. But without profit, whether in capitalism or socialism, there can be no progress. If all that is produced by labor is consumed by labor, there is nothing left.

If the laborer gets the full return of his labor, and there is no profit, then non-laborers cannot survive. Since they are non-producers they depend upon producers for their support. There must be surplus from labor to support the bureaucrats, not to mention the teachers, the armed forces, the policemen, and other necessary functionaries. Capitalism and socialism both depend on profit, the difference being who controls it and how it is distributed. Communism is totalitarian in that the distribution of profit is determined by the masters.

Communism promotes revolutionary violence to eliminate the bourgeoisie. Its morality and ethics are opposed to New Testament morality and ethics, for it engages in and encourages treachery and deceit. The ultimate objective of Communism is to dominate the world. This domination is inevitable, according to Communism's immutable economic laws of determinism. Communism is purely pragmatic, guided by the one principle that the end justifies the means. Whatever one must do to attain the objective is permissible. For example, in dialogue with a democracy such as the United States, Communists, in order to gain a hearing, claim to support freedom, for this is the principle of democracy. But when Communism actually takes over a country, freedom is suppressed.

The case for the antithetical difference between Christianity and Communism is so obvious that it hardly needs documentation. It can be and has been developed far beyond this cursory statement. What is apparent, however, is that no one can be simultaneously a Christian and a Marxist. The two cannot be mixed any more than oil and water. To accommodate Marxism to Christianity is not to alter it but to destroy it, leaving the term Marxism with no content. To accommodate Christianity to Marxism is to emasculate the faith, destroy its foundations, and render it sterile. Christianity and Communism are genuinely incompatible. No one can be a real Christian and a Marxist at the same time.

None of this should give the Christian an easy conscience about obvious social injustices. These exist and they are wrong. The believer must work for social change and true justice. But the Communist alternative is a false secular gospel, an ultimately impotent counterfeit, and a utopian dream that can never become a reality. If there are to be lasting solutions to social injustice, the solutions are not to be found in Communism.

WOMEN'S LIBERATION

One of the great contributions of Christianity to humanity has been the improvement of the condition of women. From time immemorial they have been subordinate to men and have experienced a variety of indignities. The position of women under law, even in Christian societies, was unequal. For the most part they were prohibited from owning property, making contracts, or voting. All too often they were looked upon as chattel.

In recent years, however, a tremendous wave of pressure has erupted to secure equal rights for women. In the United States this has taken the form of a constitutional amendment assuring women of the same rights as men, with no exceptions.

Part of the drive for female equality has come from the Women's Liberation Movement. In no sense can this movement be called Christian. It is secular and its leadership has been curiously devoid of the characteristics one would normally expect from Christians, male and female. Nevertheless, the existence of secular movements for women's liberation does not excuse Christian conscience from examining the question from the Christian perspective and formulating a Christian view from biblical data.

Christian women fighting for liberation fit into an entirely different category from the secular women's liberationists, and have very different objectives. Betty Friedan, author of *The Feminine Mystique,* is a non-feminine hedonist leader of women's liberation. A Smith College graduate, Phi Beta

Kappa, married and divorced, she is chairwoman of National Women's Political Caucus, and a member of the Association of Humanistic Psychology. Her views on sex are not only "progressive" and unorthodox. They are distinctly non-Christian and would shock her Jewish forebears, who based their viewpoint on the law of Moses.

Curiously, another leader in the forefront of secular women's liberation, Gloria Steinem, is also a Smith College graduate (magna cum laude) and a member of Phi Beta Kappa. As with Friedan's, there is little that is compatible with Christianity in her viewpoint. Indeed, a great deal of her thinking would have to be classified as deliberately anti-Christian.

A third well known active supporter of women's liberation is Katherine (Kate) Millett (Yoshimura), Phi Beta Kappa, magna cum laude, graduate of the University of Minnesota. A fourth is Germaine Greer, a graduate with honors of the University of Melbourne (Australia), and author of *The Female Eunuch*.

One thing these leaders of the movement share in common: they are brilliant, well-educated college and university graduates. Another common bond is their hostility to anything that could be categorized as distinctively Christian. Still another is their desire to shake off the shackles of conventional conduct in order to be free to do whatever is right in their own eyes.

In all fairness it should be stated that there are non-Christian women who take exception to the viewpoints of these high priestesses of the Movement. One articulate opponent is Midge Decter, author of *The New Chastity and Other Arguments Against Women's Liberation*. She argues that women's real difficulties do not spring from oppression —that is the denial of freedom—but from an unprecedented amount of freedom and the consequent wide range of choices.

What is significant in this continuing battle is something conveniently overlooked by the liberationists: no woman needs to become a Playboy bunny or a topless dancer; no woman must be a fornicator or an adulteress. Nor does she need to marry if she prefers a career and the celibate life. The most agonizing failure of the secular women's liberationists is that with their emphasis on liberty, they have sold out to license, and refuse to be informed of what the good life consists of as revealed in the Bible. Once they, or anybody else, have spurned the biblical ethic, they are bound to end up shipwrecked.

The existence of a women's liberation movement that is antinomian and has no concern for, or interest in, Christian liberation for women should not blind us as Christians to the rightful cry of Christian women for justice, and a re-study of their role and rightful place in God's plan of the ages.

The Christian community, which for many years pioneered among pagan peoples to improve the status of women in society, is now dragging its feet. What is required of Christians is not that they meet the approval of society but that they be faithful to their unique calling. Any survey of the role of women in the Church will reveal some amusing and amazing inconsistencies. Until now wars have been fought by men, not women. But in the missionary battle against the devil, women have been at the forefront. In the latter half of the 19th century the number of women missionaries surpassed the number of men; right now approximately 30% of all missionaries are single women—and nearly 100% of male missionaries are married. However, there are few women missionary executives.

Another strange inconsistency is that women are permitted to preach to foreign tribes as missionaries but are not often allowed to preach to their peers at home. The matter of ordaining women is controversial with many denominational leaders, yet the average Sunday School would go out of business if women stopped teaching classes. Most church choirs are heavily populated by women. But few women serve as trustees, deacons, or elders. The objections to women as deacons and elders, as well as ministers, are based most often on the Pauline injunction that women are to be silent in the church. There are some, however, who feel that Paul's command related to a specific situation and does not wholly apply today; they point out that Philip's daughters were prophetesses (Acts 21:9), as was Anna (Lk. 2:36), and that these women could not have fulfilled their offices had they been silent in church.

The narrow view that women's activities should be limited only to the home, the children, and the church is no longer adequate, having been defined and enforced by men in an earlier age. At the same time, however, Christian women have tended to accept the stereotype of themselves as servants, not leaders. Some have tired of the struggle to succeed in areas traditionally occupied by men and have given up. Evangelical women need to re-evaluate their roles, talents, and expectations—not only as church members but as human beings.

The Bible does speak rather specifically about male-female relationships for those who have been regenerated. Paul is the great advocate of Christian freedom, saying that in Jesus Christ, "There is neither Jew nor Greek, there is neither slave nor free, there is neither male nor female; for you are all one in Christ Jesus" (Gal. 3:28). Male and female Christians are members before God of the same body. They stand on the same level at the foot of the Cross. And there are no sections in heaven marked off "For Men Only."

In 1938 Dorothy Sayers spoke about Jesus' attitude toward women. He "never nagged at them, never flattered or coaxed or patronized . . . . [he] rebuked without condescension; took their questions and arguments seriously; never mapped out their sphere for them, never urged them to be feminine or jeered at them for being female; had no axe to grind and no uneasy male dignity to defend; took them as he found them and was completely unself-conscious . . . . Nobody could guess from the words and deeds of Jesus that there was anything 'funny' about woman's nature" (*Are Women Human?*, Eerdmans, 1971, p. 47).

What we need today says Letha Scanzoni, is the "vision of men and women as co-sharers of God's grace and co-workers in Christ's kingdom" (*Christianity Today,* February 2, 1973 issue, page 10). So far as individual churches and Christians are concerned, they should ask not what women as a group can do, but what a particular woman with certain talents, strengths, and weaknesses can do. The obligation is not to give "women" a chance at certain jobs, but to give a specific human being who happens to be a female the opportunity to succeed in an area to which she feels she can contribute something, even if no other woman before her has shown an interest in this area. We do not ask if men as a group can fulfill certain roles; we judge each man by what he himself accomplishes. If a woman knows, under God, that her vocation is that of wife and mother, feminists should not try to shame her into feeling unfulfilled. And if a woman knows that a career is what best suits her abilities and personality, then she should have full freedom to make that choice.

All women should enjoy the same rights as men before the law. These rights should not be abridged because of sex any more than because of color. Christian women have an added responsibility. They are not to struggle for *their* freedom only, but for the opportunity for all human beings to find freedom through enslavement to Christ.

AMERICANISM

Previously we spoke of the Christian as a member of two kingdoms: the kingdom of God and the kingdom of Caesar. This position creates tension because the Christian lives between two periods—the period of his redemption when his salvation begins, and that of consummation when his salvation is completed. Between these times he is in the world; he lives in a community and is a citizen of a nation. Everyone is a citizen of one nation or another. Because I am an American, I write from that background and context; but what is said here about America can be said with some modifications about many other nations, with the exception of totalitarian states.

Every Christian who is an American has certain responsibilities to the state. For example, he is to pay his taxes (Mt. 22:21; Rom. 13:7). Both Jesus and Paul said the Christian is to render to Caesar the things that belong to Caesar. They were living under the dominant world power of that day, the Roman Empire. Paul was a Roman citizen and proud of that fact. He did not hesitate to use his citizenship to demand his rights.

But Caesar's government was anti-Christian, thoroughly pagan, and capricious. It was to this wicked government that Christians were ordered to pay their taxes. It is, of course, quite immaterial whether the taxes are equitable or inequitable. They are to be paid and paid honestly. Neither Jesus nor Paul said that the Christian should decide whether he will or won't pay taxes depending on how the taxes are used. Rome used tax money to oppress others politically, economically, and socially. Indeed, in the Roman wars of aggression this imperial power reduced many to slavery. The slave owners even had the power to kill their slaves if they so chose.

The Vietnamese War was felt by many Americans to be

unjust. Some refused to pay their taxes, arguing that their tax money was used to carry on the war. Whether the war was just or unjust is totally beside the point. The Christian is commanded to pay his taxes whatever they are used for. He is not considered by either Jesus or Paul to be guilty of wrongdoing for paying tax money that is used for an un-Christian purpose. But he is guilty of wrongdoing if he fails to pay his taxes.

A Christian American can gladly pay his taxes without compunction, knowing as he pays them that his government, whatever its shortcomings, is far better than the ancient government of Rome or modern governments such as the Soviet Union, the People's Republic of China, and the non-Communist totalitarian countries. He can be proud of the fact that he is an American, although, as we shall see in a moment, there is an ever present danger of falling into the wrong kind of Americanism.

Paul also said that Christians are to be subject to the governing authorities (Rom. 13:1). This is a hard commandment. Again we must remember that Paul was speaking as a Roman citizen. He himself was later to be condemned to death by Caesar, to whom he appealed for justice. How can the Christian who is subject to the governing authorities be an anarchist or an advocate of violent revolution? Under no circumstances is it justified for the Christian to be an anarchist. The anarchist would do away with government, which God has ordained; and Paul says, "Therefore he who resists the authorities resists what God has appointed, and those who resist will incur judgment" (Rom 13:2).

What about the revolutionary, who resists governing authorities and would pull them down to substitute something else in their place? Certainly Paul did nothing to resist Roman authority, which was imperialistic, totalitarian, and oppressive. Nor did he foment revolution, engage in plotting to overthrow the government, or otherwise seek to instigate rebellion or civil war. Yet Paul and Jesus were revolutionaries employing a different kind of weapon. Paul exclaimed: "For though we live in the world we are not carrying on a worldly war, for the weapons of our warfare are not worldly but have divine power to destroy strongholds" (2 Cor. 10:3, 4). This indeed was a different power from that engaged in or advocated by the revolutionaries of our day. Is it not significant that Christianity nevertheless brought down the Roman Empire and did so without recourse to physical force? It was spiritual power that was responsible. Likewise, Telemachus, a single person, by the power of a dedicated life brought about an end to human slaughter by animals in the Roman Colosseum.

The Acts of the Apostles tells the story of the infant Church at work spreading the Gospel. It is a story of opposition faced and overcome, of problems met and solved. Time and again these early Christians were brought before the Roman authorities, charged with breaking the law and plotting to overthrow the Roman government. Luke in Acts "is careful to point out that the Christians were not enemies of the Empire; every time the missionaries were brought before Roman authorities they were absolved of all charges of sedition and insurrection" (Harper Study Bible, p. 1625).

Surely there is no biblical warrant for Christians to pull down the "system" in the United States. In the first place conditions in the United States are far better than those in most other countries in the world. Comparatively speaking, the United States still stands out as one of the best examples of a free people, and despite its imperfections its citizens have more justice and access to it than most other peoples around the world.

Paul argues further that "supplications, prayers, intercessions and thanksgivings be made for all men, for kings and all who are in high positions" (1 Tim. 2:2). The apostle Peter says: "Honor the emperor" (1 Pet. 2:17). This is commanded not simply when the chief of state is a good man, or of our particular party, or one whom we especially like. The president of the country is to be honored and prayed for simply because he is president. Certainly Americans have often vilified their leaders, but the Christian is not to do so.

Nations, as well as individuals, have imperfections. There is no moral ailment that individuals suffer that nations do not also suffer. They can be proud, vain, arrogant, self-seeking, arbitrary, and oppressive. All the same, they are not to be judged on the basis of their weaknesses and sins alone; whatever is good about them must be taken into account as well, and a decision arrived at on the basis of both the good and the bad. Jingoistic Americanism is a disease, a syndrome that unfortunately besets Christians as well as others.

Extreme Americanism consists in an uncritical adulation and praise of the country, a virtual worship that borders on identifying God with country and country with God. The Boy Scout motto, "For God and Country," in some measure symbolizes this attitude. Of course there is nothing wrong for the Christian to be for God and for his country. Nor is there any reason for the Christian to downgrade his country at every opportunity. What is wrong is for him to act as though America can do no wrong, to accord to it a status that may overshadow his loyalty to God. In a subtle way this is easy to do.

The attitude, "my country, right or wrong," has in it the seed of a serious heresy, suggesting a blind loyalty that refuses to face the demonic as well as the angelic in the nation. It leaves the impression that the citizen is to support wrong in much the same way that he supports right. The

Christian ought not look at America through rose-colored glasses. Rather, he should be careful to apply the same moral law to his nation as he would to the individual. Integrity, probity, and justice are as important to the nation as to the individual.

In the process of looking at America, the Christian is bound to make comparisons with other countries. In comparison it comes off both good and bad. The record of church attendance looks good. A far greater proportion of Americans go to church than do Swedes, Germans, Englishmen, Frenchmen, Danes, and Norwegians. In the use of its material resources to aid less fortunate people, the record of America after two world wars is impressive. When it comes to freedom of mobility and speech the American record is enviable. Citizens can freely leave the country and freely return. If they wish to become citizens of another country they are free to do so. They can speak what they think without being persecuted or consigned to jail. They have complete religious freedom, including the right to propagate their beliefs.

On the question of racism, however, the American record is marked by serious blemishes. Late in stopping slavery, the United States has taken a hundred years since then to bring about equality before the law. On the other hand, progress is evident. For example, Angela Davis, a self-confessed Communist who wants to destroy the American government, and who presented herself as a victim of white racism when charged with serious crimes, was given a fair trial and acquitted. In the Soviet Union or in China she would have disappeared behind prison bars, been sent to an insane asylum, or shot to death.

Much of the criticism directed against America involves matters that are relative. Hunger and poverty do not stalk the land, and the poverty so much talked about only seems bad in the light of so much affluence. But the poorest in America are infinitely better off than the poor in other countries. One need only travel to Dacca in Bangladesh, or to Bombay and Calcutta in India, to realize the vast gap between their poor and the poor in America. Poverty in this context is relative, and America's poor would be considered fairly affluent in other places. This is not to deny the existence or support the continuance of poverty in America. Christian conscience has always concerned itself with the indigent; Christians for centuries have been in the forefront of the work to ameliorate living conditions and eradicate poverty.

The automobile sticker, "America: Love It or Leave It," is a signpost of Americanism that is off base. This embodies the notion of uncritical acceptance and tacit approval of the country, which is a false attitude from the biblical perspective. The Christian citizen will love America. But true love is realistic. It sees the faults as well as the strengths, works for the elimination of evil, of the demonic, and seeks to improve the situation. It does not gloss over the defects. But at the same time it does not become anti-American, which is a far worse evil than the wrong kind of Americanism.

The Christian sees the need for national repentance, for national confession of sin, for restitution where needed, and for forsaking whatever may hinder the worship of God. He prays for his nation and for those in authority over him, while at the same time voting and working within the political establishment to make his Christian convictions known.

As we have mentioned in another connection earlier, the great problem for the Christian comes when Caesar's law conflicts with God's law. When this state of affairs arises the Christian candidly puts God in first place. Caesar is subject to God; America takes second place in the kingdom of God. When Caesar usurps God's prerogatives the Christian must obey God, not Caesar. He must refuse to obey any order or any law that negates God's laws. What does this mean?

It does not mean that the Christian who opposed America's involvement in Vietnam had any right to engage in sabotage, to bomb Selective Service offices, to rifle their files and pour blood over them. He would have had no right to steal confidential government papers in the excuse that they should never have been made confidential in the first place. He would have had no right to spy for another nation or be a traitor. However, he does have the God-given right to refuse to obey demands that conflict with God's law, and be willing to pay whatever penalty results from his disobedience.

In the Old Testament David refused to touch Saul when he had him at his mercy because he was the Lord's anointed. The Roman government could not make the Christians of the early church worship the emperor or offer sacrifices to idols or even eat meat offered to idols. They preferred death to disobedience to God, and the blood of the martyrs was the seed of the Church.

The Christian will be a good citizen; he will obey his country's laws and respect the authorities. But he will put God first and Caesar second. No nation has ever failed to prosper when its people put God first and their country second. The best way for any citizen to love his country and to serve it well is to do this very thing.

Is there some way we can sum up this whole business of Christian personal and social ethics? We have already spoken of the law of love. Perhaps we can conclude with that law as it was used by St. Augustine, who said, "Love God and do what you want." What he had in mind is obvious: the man who loves God will want to do the will of God. What he wants is what God wants. Here is the happiest arrangement of all: the man who truly loves God is doing what God wants and what he himself wants.

It is possible for a Christian to do the will of God unwillingly, in which case he is doing only what God wants, not what he himself wants. This means he does not truly love God; because he does not do what he really wants to do he cannot be a contented man whose heart is free from all care and at leisure from self. But when he not only does God's will but chooses that will because it is his will too, then, wonder of wonders, the peace that passes understanding is his, and the Savior's word of commendation shall resound through the halls of heaven: "Well done, good and faithful servant."

X. LIFE IN THE SPIRIT—THE ANTIDOTE TO WORLDLINESS

There are three things yet to be done when considering the Christian's walk in the world. They are: (1) to suggest guidelines for believers which they can apply to practical problems in order to make right decisions; (2) to show how the believer can gain ascendancy over worldliness; and (3) to describe what life in the Spirit is like and how it is obtained. There is some overlap in the last two.

In our advanced technological age we have tests for just about everything. We have tire gauges to determine if the air pressure is correct. We have machines by which we can test the tubes in our radios and TV sets, to see if they are functioning. Before the American astronauts went to the moon, the space ships, the rockets, and all the equipment were put through a dry run to be sure they were functioning properly and would work when the launching time came. In an analogous fashion there are tests that can be applied to questions of Christian conduct which will enable believers to decide what they ought to do.

Before any tests are proposed there is one preceding decision that must be made. Knowing what to do is one thing. Doing it is another. There is little use in deciding what to do if the will is lacking to do it after the choice is made. The Christian, therefore, should not ask the question, "What ought I to do?" unless he has first decided that he will do the will of God before he knows what that will is. He must be willing to do God's will whether he likes it or not, and whether or not it seems suitable and expedient. Indeed, doing the right thing may be very costly, and to the coldly calculating mind it may appear to be the height of foolishness. But the "foolishness" of God is wiser than the wisdom of men, and what does not make sense to the world makes a great deal of sense in the kingdom of God.

Guidelines are really valuable only to those who have a right relationship to God, who really want to know the will of God in their ethical situations. The Bible does not pretend to offer quick and easy answers to the choices the Christian must make. It does lay down some very specific injunctions, some of which we have examined; but there are far more decisions the Christian is called upon to make about which the Bible says nothing in particular. This does not mean that the Bible affords him no help. There are tests that can be used which will enable him, with the help of the Holy Spirit, to know what he should do. Here are seven suggested guidelines that have been helpful to many other Christians when called upon to make decisions.

1. *Is there any clear teaching about it in the Bible?* The Word of God commands some things and forbids others. Thus, for example, men are commanded to love their wives. What they are commanded to do they ought to do. Christians are commanded to love their enemies. Therefore they must do so. Just as there are positive commands concerning things they ought to do, so there are negative commands concerning things they are not to do. They are not to gossip, fornicate, commit adultery, lie, cheat, or steal. Wherever there is a clear teaching of what they should or should not

do, believers are to obey it. Immediate and unconditional obedience lies at the heart of Christian commitment. But for the many things that have to be decided, about which the Bible affords no immediate or direct guidance, there are other ways to determine what God wants done.

2. *What would Jesus do?* The Apostle Peter said "Christ also suffered for us, leaving us an example, that [we] should follow his steps" (1 Pet. 2:21). To ask what Jesus would do in a similar situation is to answer the question in many instances. Most Christians have a clear idea of the kind of person Jesus was and how he would have acted. If they apply this test when making decisions it will clarify things greatly. Jesus put others first; he came to serve, not to be ministered to; he sought first the kingdom of God and his righteousness; he was humble and not self-seeking. The very character of Jesus, the kind of person he was, and the life he lived are bound to be of help to believers as they decide what they ought to do.

3. *To what is your heart attached?* Does God have second place in your life, or does he have all of you at all times? The worldly person has a heart that is not wholly committed to God; it is attached to something else first. To love something else more than God, however good and laudable it may be, is worldliness. The man who puts himself, or his wife, or his children first, and whose life is otherwise spotless, is already a worldling. The world is the world because it always puts something ahead of God, and this is idolatry. Paul's admonition for believers to present their bodies as living sacrifices (Rom. 12:1-2) makes the distinction clear. Christ himself did the same with the Apostle Peter who had denied Jesus three times before the crucifixion. Following the resurrection Jesus addressed a question to Peter as he ate the breakfast prepared by the Lord: "Lovest thou me more than these?" (John 21:15). It is

unclear, perhaps purposely so, what the word "these" refers to. Did Jesus mean "Do you love me more than you love the other disciples?" or "Do you love me more than you love your boats and nets?" It really makes little difference which one we choose. Clearly Jesus was asking whether there was anything that Peter loved more than he loved Jesus. When Peter replied that he loved Him, Jesus said, "Feed my lambs." The correlation is obvious: commitment to the person of Jesus, which is primary, must be followed by the outworking of that commitment in the drama of everyday life and its nitty-gritty decisions.

4. *What is the spirit or the atmosphere of the thing?* The context surrounding every decision is important. The story is told of a Sunday school teacher and a bartender who at the last moment boarded the wrong boats for a picnic on Lake Michigan. The Sunday school teacher returned from the bartenders' outing feeling like he had been in hell, and the bartender returned from the Sunday school outing feeling like he had been in hell. There are places the believer should not go and things he should not do because the atmosphere is not conducive to Christian witness and personal development. He ought not go around with gangsters and thieves, nor have "fellowship with unfruitful works of darkness" (Eph. 5:11). Indeed, he is commanded to "cast off the works of darkness" (Rom. 13:12). To avoid all contact with evil is impossible, but to conform to it or to be its accomplice is to partake of its spirit or atmosphere. Paul told the Corinthians not to be "unequally yoked together with unbelievers" (2 Cor. 6:14). The Christian young person who does not date unbelievers won't marry them. The Christian will not have for his most intimate friends those who do not know his God.

5. *Will it help or harm your Christian life and walk?* The good is the enemy of the best. Reading a certain book or

newspaper, or watching a TV program may do no harm to my Christian life. But there may be better books that should be read and different TV programs that should be watched. The fact that something may do no harm is not enough; it ought to help one's life and walk. Of course there is a place in the Christian life for entertainment, relaxation, sports. It is good for people to play basketball, for example, or cheer for their favorite team. There is a time to play games, do nothing, or even just to sleep. Some Christians get cranky for want of sleep, not because of spiritual backsliding. The Christian of all people should avoid being lopsided. But choices should be made with an eye to their usefulness to the Christian life, having in mind the goal of being a well-read, well-rounded, knowledgeable person who can handle himself in a great variety of life situations (see Eph. 5:8, 9).

6. *How will it influence and affect others?* No man lives or dies to himself. All of life is interrelated; a man's choices affect his wife, his children, his friends, his church, his country. Therefore he must consider what his decisions will mean to a variety of people; he can do things that possibly will ruin his testimony before others. If a Christian athlete is a poor sport, this may ruin his Christian witness to unbelieving athletes who, even though not Christian, would exhibit a high degree of good sportsmanship. The Christian golfer who doesn't keep his score right may find his testimony worthless to an unregenerate man who would never cheat on the golf course. Moreover, the Christian might feel free to do something that might not harm him but which might still harm someone else or cause him to stumble. Every Christian is called to be an example to others. He cannot enjoy the luxury of doing only what pleases himself, for the believer is not only a bond slave to Jesus Christ: Paul says Christians are "your servants (bondmen) for Jesus' sake" (2 Cor. 3:5).

7. *If there is doubt, don't.* Giving God the benefit of any doubt is a good principle to follow. "Whatsoever is not of faith is sin" (Rom. 14:23). If, therefore, the Christian proposes to do something that leaves him with constraint in his conscience and a sense of uneasiness in his heart, he had better stop then and there. A good conscience is a free conscience. When the Christian has been led of the Spirit of God in his decision he has a good conscience and a sense of inward release. He is free to carry out what he has determined to do. If, however, after the Bible has been read, prayer offered, friends consulted, and the soul searched, the Christian is still unclear in his mind as to what he ought to do, he should give up his plan and forget it, or at least wait quietly for some go ahead signal. But he will not move forward until he knows he should.

The Christian must walk in the world and yet not be conformed to the world's practices (Rom. 12:2). This walk is the Christian's warfare (1 Tim. 6:12). Is he doomed to perpetual defeat or is there the possibility of victory for him along the route? Must he succumb to the temptations on the road to the celestial city or can he resist sin, live a holy life, please God, and stand unashamed with head erect? If at every turn defeat is certain, then there would be no adequate reason for God to command righteousness, forbid sin, or urge men to live for him. These things make sense only when it is possible for the Christian to enjoy some kind of holy walk, resisting sin and the blandishments of Satan.

One thing God guarantees: so long as the believer is in the world he will have tribulation (John 16:33). This is his lot and is inescapable. Trouble is chronic; there will always be circumstances that distress him, temptations that assault him, obstacles that challenge him. The more he identifies himself with Christ and gets involved in his work, the more this will be true. It is important to distinguish the source of some of the believer's trials. The trials are three in number. First, he experiences the common problems of life that beset all men alike simply because they are alive. These are human problems that both believers and non-believers experience. All men are subject to sickness, are required to labor in order to live, have to provide for wives and children, must find shelter from the weather. While tribulation can come for the Christian through these common experiences of life, they are not in themselves the tribulation of which Jesus is speaking. Tribulation goes far beyond these common problems.

In addition to the inconveniences all men experience, the believer is subject to assaults from Satan, the archenemy of his soul (1 Pet. 5:8). Satan does not bother to attack those who already belong to him. He uses a reverse strategy: he often works to keep them satisfied and content. He gives them the desires of their hearts; desires, of course, that are consistent with this life and world view, not God's. Supplied with what they want, they are lulled to sleep as they move irresistibly, albeit willingly, to their doom. Not so with believers. Satan goes to work on them—hard. He puts every conceivable temptation in their way. No red-garbed personage sporting horns and armed with a pitchfork, popular as that medieval picture may be, he comes under the guise of an angel of light (2 Cor. 11:14). He probes for weak points, using every device calculated to seduce the people of God. He knows, for example, that Christians just don't go out and commit adultery or murder suddenly. Long before they make these choices Satan softens them up and conditions them for the big sins by breaking down the barriers. Small sins, untended and unconfessed, open the gates to more and larger and grosser sins. This process is as insidious as it is subtle.

The experience of Samson illustrates very graphically how backsliding takes place. Erosion occurred in his life gradually but persistently until the moment came when God withdrew his presence from him. A Nazarite from his mother's womb, Samson was a man to whom God had given strength and on whose ministry the benediction of God rested. However, when he disclosed the secret of his power to Delilah his downfall came. She cut his hair contrary to his Nazarite vow and his strength left him. But he did not know it. When she told him that the Philistines were upon him, he said: "I will go out as at other times before, and shake myself" (Judges 16:20). Then comes the clincher: "he wist not that the Lord was departed from him" (Judges 16:20). God was gone from his life and he didn't even know it! This is the way Satan works.

As if the darts of Satan were not enough, the Christian also experiences what God himself sends to add appreciably to his difficulties. God's purpose is the opposite of Satan's. God works to fit men for heaven; Satan works to fit men for hell. Making a Christian fit for heaven is no easy task; it involves conforming him to the image of Jesus Christ, making him like the Lord himself. God sends all manner of things into the life of the believer in order to conform him to the image of Jesus. Many of these experiences are painful, and some of them do not always seem to make sense. At times God appears to be most severe and has to perform radical surgery. Sometimes he sends a Christian through a dark night of the soul via highways of cut stones that lacerate the feet. The hymn writer caught the purpose, as we should, in these words:

> Shall Jesus bear the cross alone
> And all the world go free?
> No! There's a cross for everyone
> And there's a cross for me.

Crossbearing is God's gift to his children, not to punish them, but to purify them; it is not a token of God's wrath but of his chastening and correcting love. The end God has in mind is good, but getting to the goal can be searing, scalding, and heart-breaking. At the end of the road is sainthood.

Sainthood has to do with sanctification. Here we come into an area of theology that has pitfalls. Christians have differed widely in their views about sanctification, probably because Scripture itself seems to introduce a paradox.

There are three biblical doctrines that are important here: justification, sanctification, and glorification. The great teaching of the Bible deals with the question of how a man is saved. Both the Old and the New Testaments teach that men are justified by faith (Gal. 3:24; Hab. 2:4 and Rom. 1:17). What does this mean?

As we have already said, man is declared to be righteous when he is justified. He is not righteous in himself, but has the righteousness of Christ imputed to him or laid to his account (Rom. 4:6-8). God has promised that salvation, which is progressive, will be completed when the believer is glorified (Rom. 8:30). At that time he will be perfectly holy. Between justification and glorification lies the time of sanctification which lasts from the moment a man is regenerated and justified until death. This is to be followed at the end of the age by the resurrection from the dead, at which time the believer is made perfect in holiness, or glorified.

The thorny question is whether it is possible for the Christian to attain a life of holiness while he remains in the flesh. Through all the centuries of the Christian church God's people have sought to attain holiness. They have sought holiness because the Bible commands it. Thus Hebrews 12:14 says, "Strive for peace with all men, and for the holiness without which no one will see the Lord."

Holiness must be understood not merely as a state or a

condition but as having to do with one's daily life. It asks the question of whether the believer can live even for a single day without committing sin. How this question is answered makes a very considerable difference in one's attitude toward Christian life and conduct. It also brings the earnest Christian to a decision as to how he understands and interprets the Bible at this point.

Before deciding whether any Christian can or does live a life of sinlessness one fact must be driven home. Sinful man is justified by faith through the grace of God (Eph. 2:8, 9). This means his works can never save him, for if salvation were to be earned by works no one would be saved. But it is likewise true that no one is kept in the state of salvation by works either. No one can work to become saved and no one can work to remain saved. Therefore even if man lived a wholly sinless life in which he neither thought, said, nor did anything sinful, it still would have nothing whatever to do with his being justified or his remaining justified.

Charles G. Finney's friend, John Morgan, wrote in his *Systematic Theology* that "It is admitted by all, except utter antinomians, that some degree of holiness or conformity to the divine law is indispensable to acceptance with God." If this is true, then works have become an essential part of justification. It is no longer "sola fide," i.e., faith alone. It is now faith plus works. Grace has then ceased to be grace. Let it therefore be said that no one ever has or ever will be acceptable to God on the basis of conformity to the divine law. Man is justified by faith alone apart from works. The attainment of any degree of holiness as a necessary condition of being justified must be ruled out.

This brings us to the second aspect of holiness (sanctification) in relation to justification. "Is it necessary to attain some degree of holiness in order to remain justified?" Once a man says that any degree of holiness is necessary in order to remain saved, wholly apart from sinless perfection, he has in effect nullified the doctrine of grace and has fallen into the error of saying that man is saved by grace through faith but kept by works. Since the Bible excludes works as a necessary part of being justified or remaining justified, let no one suppose that works have anything to do with the believer's legal standing before God.

If the Christian is not saved or kept by works or by his holiness, is it still possible for the Christian to attain to some degree of holiness or even to attain sinless perfection in this life?

No one will deny that, at the very least, sanctification does mean the attainment of some degree of holiness. Sanctification is progressive, by which is meant that the believer is to die to sin and live to righteousness. He is to put off the old man and to put on the new man (Col. 3:1 ff.). Day by day he is being conformed to the image of Jesus Christ.

From the biblical data it is inconceivable to suppose that the man who has been justified will continue to live the same kind of life or perform the same kind of deeds as he did before he was converted. The salvation process includes more than justification and regeneration; it goes on to sanctification, which is also the work of God in the believer's life. The believer is urged to work out what God is working in him (Phil. 2:12, 13). Sanctification is God at work, making the believer what he ought to be. If anyone professes Christianity without that profession being followed by a radical transformation in his life, we can assume he has not had a genuine saving experience.

The biblical doctrine of salvation includes all of the other doctrines which are part of it: repentance, faith, justification, regeneration, sanctification, glorification. We can say that we have been saved, we are being saved, and we will be saved. So also we can say we have been sanctified, we are being sanctified, and we will be sanctified. Positionally we have already been sanctified; in God's sight it is as if we are already holy. But we are also being sanctified. This is a lifelong process by which we gradually become more and more conformed to the life of the Lord Jesus. At last the final and full sanctification will take place when the believer is glorified.

We have already described what worldliness is. It is a lack of holiness. If the Christian is not to be worldly then of necessity he must be holy. If he is to be what God wants him to be, he must be Spirit-filled. There is a definite and perceptible difference between a carnal Christian and a spiritual one. How does one become a spiritual Christian? It is at this point that there is an apparent paradox. Holiness or sanctification is the work of God and of the Christian. He has become a new creation in Christ Jesus. Here and now some of what was lost in the fall of Adam has been restored. At last all that was lost will be recovered, but not while the believer is still in the flesh.

Before the Christian was saved he was a worldling. After he is saved he is called upon to stop being a worldling, for God is at work in his life and he is called upon to respond to God. This has nothing to do with his justification but with sanctification. How does the believer become sanctified? How does he become Spirit-filled?

The Christian can be an overcomer. He can, by God's grace, put off the old man. He can slough off the self-style, the life of carnality, the life of depression and despair. He can have the fruit of the Spirit—love, joy, peace, patience, kindness, goodness, faithfulness, gentleness, and self-control (Gal. 5:22). This comes when the believer is filled with the Spirit. There are four steps that need to be followed by the Christian.

1. *He must deal with the sin question.* Before anyone can be filled with the Spirit he first must be emptied. You can't put anything into a cup that is already full. Nor can the Holy Spirit fill the heart that is already occupied by something else. Whatever keeps the Holy Spirit from filling the heart must be removed. This means that the sin question has to be dealt with. The heart must be prepared for the Holy Spirit's fulness by being cleansed from known sin. Because no one is exactly like anybody else, each will have his own sin problem. Perhaps it is some besetting sin of the flesh, some filthy habit that can't be shaken. Maybe it is some defilement of the mind, an impurity that has corroded the thought life. Maybe it is spiritual sin like doubt or unbelief. Whatever the sins are, they have to be confessed. God must be allowed to search the heart and bring conviction of sin. But conviction is not enough. It must be accompanied by contrition, a godly sorrow for sin.

The means of cleansing from sin is the blood of Jesus Christ. John says, "The blood of Jesus Christ his Son cleanseth us from all sin" (1 John 1:7). Sins have to be put under the cleansing blood of Jesus Christ. There is no other means. Man cannot atone for his own sins. Forgiveness is not possible any other way. Thus, whoever would know holiness must be cleansed by the blood of Jesus. What is the method by which sins are put under the cleansing blood?

The method of cleansing is confession. "If we confess our sins, he is faithful and just to forgive us our sins, and to cleanse us from all unrighteousness" (1 John 1:9). It is not enough to say, "Forgive me all my sins." Specific sins need to be enumerated and repented of—the lack of love, the bitter word, the distrust of God, the lie, the adulterous thought. The earnest believer needs to confess the particular sins in his life he knows about so well. He confesses them in order to put them under the covering of Christ's blood.

All known sin must be confessed. Let there be no known dregs left, no little idols still perched on any shelf of the heart. Every sin has to go, every known burden of the heart needs to be rolled away. Only when the heart is emptied of *known* sin by confession, followed by cleansing, is the Christian ready for the next step.

2. *He must surrender himself.* God wants the believer's heart. He wants each of his children to give himself to him freely, volitionally, once and forever. It is not an act that needs to be repeated, although it may be reaffirmed. In marriage, one's vows can be reaffirmed but need not be repeated. No one needs to be married twice. Once does it. So with surrender. To do it once is to do it forever. In doing it the Christian presents himself to God Almighty (Rom. 12:1, 2). He gives God the undivided possession and control of his life. From that moment on he is not his own. He acknowledges that he has been bought with a price, and the only true way he can respond to the purchase is to glorify God by turning his body over to the one who has redeemed him.

The moment of surrender is no less solemn than that moment of conversion when a man is justified and born from above. Every Christian must know Christ not only as Saviour but also as Lord. Surrender has to do with the Lordship of Christ. In theory Christ should be both Saviour and Lord from the moment a man has been born from above. The ideal does not always occur then. Justification leads to sanctification. At the heart of sanctification lies the necessity of surrender when the believer gives himself in principle wholly over to God. Great care is needed here to avoid the use of absolutes. To do something in principle is not the same as to do something which is free from all taint and stain. For a man to give himself to his profession, say medicine or law, is to devote himself to it in principle as much as he is able. But it will not be perfect.

Abraham presented his son Isaac to God on the altar of sacrifice (Gen. 22:9-14). There undoubtedly were reservations and qualifications in his mind when he did so. His act was not a perfect act. But in principle, despite any imperfections, he presented his son to God. One clue to the imperfection of Abraham's offering is suggested in Hebrews 11:19. "He considered that God was able to raise men even from the dead." He believed that God would give Isaac back to him after he had killed him. Clearly Abraham might have had a different viewpoint if he had been convinced that Isaac, once dead, would not be revivified. The passage even suggests that Abraham was willing to lose Isaac forever, but not without reservation. The only perfect acts of presentation were performed by God the Father and Jesus the Son. The Father gave the Son to Calvary's cross with no reservations of any kind. Jesus gave himself to the Father's will with no reservations.

We give ourselves to God with doubts, with reservations, with hesitation. It is not done perfectly, but however imperfectly it is done, God accepts the intention in principle. Paul says to present our bodies (Rom. 12:1, 2)—and we do, but only because God by his Spirit gives us liberty and grace to do it. It is well to avoid the language of "absolute surrender," since we are still in the flesh; and although we make the presentation and it is accepted by God, it is far from absolute.

The act of surrender may or may not be an emotional experience; there may or may not be tears of joy. It is essentially a volitional act, an act of will, a choice or a decision that signals a new relationship. It is a definite act that does not need to be repeated, although it may be reaffirmed. To know at that time or at any future time what all the consequences will be is impossible. Surrender has nothing whatever to do with the question of vocational (or full-time) Christian service, but simply means that the surrendered person is now at God's disposal, in principle, for him to do with as he pleases. What that person becomes or where he serves is secondary. What is primary is that he is where God wants him to be and doing what God has appointed for him.

The exchanged (or surrendered) life is not an impoverished life. No one loses anything worthwhile by making this decision. Is that man a fool who gladly gives up what he can't keep, to gain what he can't lose? The wisest thing anyone can do to further his own best interests and his ultimate good is to let go of his life to God.

3. *He must ask God to fill him with his Spirit*. When the sin question has been taken care of and the life presented to God, then, and then only, should the Christian ask to be filled with the Holy Spirit. Cleansing and surrender are prerequisites to filling. Paul admonished the Ephesians: "Be not drunk with wine, wherein is excess; but be filled with the Spirit" (Eph. 5:18). Jesus promised that those who ask receive, those who seek find, those who knock have it opened to them. Since it is the will of God for his people to be filled with his Spirit, the Christian can be sure he will be filled if the required conditions are met. The prayer is a simple one: "Lord, fill me with your Holy Spirit."

4. *He must accept the filling*. Just as the believer is saved by faith, so he walks by faith. By faith he believes that God has filled him with his Holy Spirit, and having received the filling by faith he goes out to live as one filled. When a man has been married he then goes out to conduct himself and to live as a married man. Jesus healed a man whose arm was paralyzed. He commanded him to reach forth with it. Now if there is anything paralysis makes impossible it is to

use the affected limb. Yet when the man attempted to do the apparently impossible he succeeded. His arm was healed. No one can walk in the power of the Spirit on his own. But when he reaches forth to do so the power is there, the Holy Spirit is present, and the impossible is done.

When the believer is filled with the Holy Spirit he is sensitized to sin. First he recognizes some things in his life to be sin that before were not regarded as sinful at all. Second, the Holy Spirit brings conviction of sin to the believer in sharper and more forceful ways than before. Thus he not only sees as sin things that formerly meant nothing, but his conscience hurts him more and he suffers more when sins go untended. Third, the Holy Spirit gives him added power by which he is able to resist temptation when it comes and to cease doing some things that formerly he was unable to overcome. He is given power to put to death what is earthly in him (Col. 3:5). This includes anger, wrath, malice, slander, foul talk, and lying.

Being filled with the Holy Spirit does not mean that the believer will never again tell a lie, get angry, gossip, experience unclean desires, or fall into a hundred kindred pitfalls. If this is true and he does some of these things, how then has he ceased to be worldly? 1 John 3:9 throws some light on this question. From the Greek tenses the passage might well be translated, "Whoever is born of God does not make sin the practice of his life." 1 John 1:8 states that "If we say we have no sin, we deceive ourselves, and the truth is not in us." Therefore John could not then say that God's children do not or cannot sin. But they need not make sin the practice of life.

The testimony of the Apostle Paul points up the dilemma we all face and the paradox we encounter. In Romans he carefully concludes that Jew and Gentile alike are guilty and fall under the condemnation of God. The conclusion that all men are guilty naturally includes himself. Yet in Philippians 2:6 he says that "as to the righteousness under the law (he was) blameless." He is both blameless and guilty. Following this reasoning the best of all believers is both saint and sinner. The work of God in sanctification is to make the believer less of a sinner and more of a saint. However much of a saint he becomes, he is still a sinner while in the flesh. He is both justified and sanctified but he is not yet completely perfect and he is not yet holy. He waits to occupy heaven, to which he has a title deed, and he inclines his heart toward that perfection he has not yet attained. But he lives in hope, with the knowledge and expectation that he will be saved and will become sinless.

Scripture everywhere sets up the ideal of what we ought to be, assuring us that we will become what we ought to be. But until this life is ended the believer is always in the process of becoming. He never fully arrives in this life. But the Spirit-filled Christian is making progress, does have power to resist what he formerly gave in to, and does have victory after victory in the struggle against sin and Satan.

There is the kingdom of grace and the kingdom of glory. Sinners enter the kingdom of grace; only the sinless enter the kingdom of glory. The people of God in the kingdom of grace long for holiness, feel the awfulness of their sins, and cry to God for his consolation and support. They delight in God's law after the inward man (Rom. 7:22-25). They would rather die than commit a known sin. Yet they know that even their best acts are unworthy before God, and they mourn because they never fully meet God's requirements of holiness.

Here is the believer's tension: he is in the world but not of the world. He is resisting the world and reaching out toward holiness. He is dying more and more to self and sin, even as he is living more and more to God and holiness.

To the extent that he walks in the Spirit he will not fulfill the lusts of the flesh. He is putting on the Lord Jesus Christ and waiting with patience for the full realization of all that God has promised him. Salvation is nearer to him now than when he first believed. The night is far gone, the day is at hand (Rom. 13:11, 12). Fight the good fight. Aim at righteousness, godliness, faith, love, steadfastness, gentleness (1 Tim. 6:12, 11). For the believer who does this is well pleasing to the Master and blameless in the Master's sight.

As soon as anyone says that no believer ever reaches a state of sinless perfection in this life, some people quickly jump to the wrong conclusions: since sinful and imperfect people get into heaven, then it really makes little difference whether Christians strive to live holy lives. They often argue that this leads to antinomianism, with the corollary dogma, "sin that grace may abound." This antinomian idea is offensive to holiness people, who are generally Arminian rather than Calvinist, and who, along with their perfectionism, teach that the Christian can fall from grace by sinning since he is a free creature. They oppose the idea of the perseverance of the saints, otherwise known as eternal security (John 10:27-30).

If the believer can lose his salvation, then grace has ceased to be grace alone (sola gratia), and faith plus works once more enters the picture (Rom. 3:27 ff.). What makes this even more difficult is the argument of the writer to the Hebrews, that if it were possible for men to lose their salvation (he is not saying it is possible), it would be impossible to get it back again since this would be to crucify Christ the second time. He died for men once, not twice. Thus if those for whom Christ died once were to fall from grace, there is no further hope for them. They can enter into salvation once through faith, but not twice. But Arminian doctrine allows the possibility of men falling from grace: they can lose and then regain their salvation many times (Heb. 6:1-6).

It is within this context that we must answer the question, "Why should the Christian who knows he will never be perfected, yet saved, feel constrained to live a holy life?" First, we need to recall that whenever God states what will happen when men obey him, he also states what will happen to them if they disobey.

The Jews were forewarned of the consequences of disobedience as well as of the blessings of obedience (see,e.g., Deut. 28:15-20). Adam was forewarned of the consequences of disobedience. The Gospel everywhere proclaims that when men come to God through faith in Jesus Christ they will be saved. But it also warns men that their refusal of salvation will result in condemnation and everlasting separation from the presence of God. Moreover, God also warns the believer of the consequences that come as a result of his failure to live a holy life. The benefit of a holy life is obvious—felicity in the presence of God forever. But what happens to the believer who gets into heaven (inherits eternal life) even though his life has been far from holy? When the answer to this question is understood the believer will be greatly concerned about the life of holiness, and will avail himself of all the divine resources which will enable him to attain holiness in this life to the highest degree possible.

There is the judgment of the great white throne (Rev. 20:11 ff.). No believer will appear at this judgment, only the unsaved. But there is a second judgment, the believer's judgment. This is not a judgment of life and death, for that issue has already been settled. The believer has been justified and has been given a title deed to heaven. The believer's judgment, then, has nothing whatever to do with his standing before God, his righteousness, but has to do with the believer's works.

Paul says, "So then every one of us shall give account of himself to God" (Rom. 14:2). "We must appear before the judgment seat of Christ; that every one may receive the things done in his body, according to that he hath done, whether it be good or bad" (2 Cor. 5:10).

The judgment seat of Christ is the place before which the believer comes. The time of this judgment is after the resurrection of all believers, when they have received their immortal and incorruptible bodies. The purpose of the judgment is to evaluate the works they have done after they have been saved. The decision in this judgment has for its purpose the handing out of rewards for faithfulness or the withholding of rewards for unfaithfulness. This is the reason why the attainment of holiness in this life of probation is of such importance to the Christian. Salvation, or admission to God's presence, is by unearned grace, not by merit. But the reward in heaven is earned by works. Rewards are the product of effort and labor; even here, however, grace is involved. The best of the believer's works are defective and are not, therefore, meritorious. But God judges the intent of the heart (1 Kings 8:17-19). Self-seeking desire for heavenly rewards has no proper place in the Christian's motivation, since he no longer lives for himself, but for Christ who died for him (2 Cor. 5:15). The rewards have value as a demonstration of the grace and righteousness of God. The believer desires them only as a display of the glory of God.

The Apostle Paul wrote to the Corinthian church about the matter of rewards, saying that the foundation of the Christian life is Jesus Christ. Every Christian builds a habitation on this foundation. Some use wood, hay, and stubble as building materials; others use gold, silver, and precious stones. Each man's *work* will become manifest. It will be tested by fire. "If the *work* which any man has built on the foundation survives, he will receive a reward. If any man's work is burned up, he will suffer loss, though he himself will be saved, but only as through fire" (1 Cor. 3:10 ff.).

Simple honesty demands that every Christian accept truth whether it is palatable or not, and whether he likes it or not. One of these truths is that however much the Christian yearns for perfection he will not attain it in this life. The second is that true grace and faith never fail in this life to produce good works, but they never relate to justification. The third is that the believer must strive for holiness or life in the Holy Spirit. The fourth is that every believer faces the eventual judgment of Christ, and this judgment may be adverse. If so, it is his own fault and he has no one to blame except himself.

The most unpalatable truth of all for the Christian is that there are some believers who get into heaven with the smell of smoke on their garments, empty-handed, and without anything durable to present to Christ. The test of fire destroys what they have built on the foundation of Jesus Christ. This ought not to be true. It need not be true. Life in the Spirit, the life of victory, is the life of good works, which means being something and doing something for God's glory. Faced with the necessity of going through the believer's judgment, every Christian should order his life so as to make it well-pleasing to God. He must forsake worldliness, for to be worldly or to cling to worldliness is the surest guarantee of entering heaven empty-handed. The life of victory, the life in the Spirit, is to live for God. This insures that the believer will go through the judgment with a building that will withstand the heat of the fire and emerge as a glorious token of the believer's devotion to holiness, which glorifies Christ the Redeemer.

XI. THE CHURCH AND THE WORLD

God's plan of the ages can be broken down into the old and the new covenants, represented by the Old and the New Testament Scriptures. The old covenant has to do with Israel, the Levitical priesthood, the temple and its sacrifices. The new covenant fulfills the old covenant, which was preparatory, transitory, to be superseded when Jesus Christ came and fulfilled his mission. Even as Israel was at the center of the Old Testament (testament means covenant), so the Church is at the heart of the New Testament. Before discussing the Church and its relationship to the world, a preliminary word about Israel and the old covenant will be helpful.

At the center of God's plan lay the Cross of Calvary. Prior to that event all history was preparation for it; subsequently all history looks back to it. God called Abraham to be the father of a covenant people who were to be separated to God (Gen. 12:2, 3, 7; 13:14-17). The sign and seal of the covenant was circumcision (Gen. 17:9, 10). Israel was to be a separated people distinguishable from all the nations around them. They were promised a land, sovereignty, a large population, adequate food, and divine protection. They were prohibited from intermarriage with the heathen (Ex. 34:15, 16). They were given a system of personal and social ethics regulating their relationship to God and to each other (see the book of Leviticus). God did not choose to reveal all of his plan to them at one time; even that which he did reveal was sometimes veiled. Instead his revelation was progressive. He did specify nevertheless that there was a Messiah who was to come (Isa. 9:6). There is a sense in which God's purpose for Israel was different from God's purpose for the Church: Israel was to be separated physically from the heathen; the Church was to be in the world.

The ideal purpose of God for Israel was never fulfilled. They were a disobedient people who intermingled and intermarried with the heathen, backslid, and eventually became apostate. God did not forsake his people despite their backsliding; he did not destroy them in the wilderness even though they engaged in licentious conduct and demanded that Aaron manufacture idols (see Ex. 32). They apostatized repeatedly in the time of the Judges, and God delivered them into the hands of oppressors as a means of chastening them. Still later God sent his people into the Babylonian captivity for seventy years. At last the full measure of judgment was executed on Israel in the dispersion (diaspora), even as it had been foretold in Deuteronomy 28:58 ff.

But God's judgment on Israel and their dispersion among the nations of the world did not take place before the redemptive plan of God in the incarnation had been fulfilled.

God knew from eternity how Israel would react and how Israel would fall. His redemptive purpose, however, was not limited to Israel only, but embraced the whole world (the God of the whole earth shall he be called [Is. 54:5]). The Gentiles were definitely included in the plan of God.

The new covenant in a special way deals with the calling out of the Gentiles (Rom. 11:11 ff.). This calling out process is channeled, in the plan of God, through the Church, the *ecclesia,* which comprises the called-out ones. What is the Church, what is its function or mission, and what is its destiny?

The Church is the bride of the Lord Jesus Christ; he is the bridegroom (Rev. 19:9). The Church is also called his body (Eph. 1:22, 23). Every Christian is a member of that body (Eph. 5:30). The Church itself has Jesus Christ as its foundation. "For other foundation can no man lay than that is laid, which is Jesus Christ" (1 Cor. 3:11). Men enter the Church via the new birth, or regeneration. This occurs when they have been declared righteous by God through their faith. The Church is related to a still larger phenomenon, the kingdom of God, which is past, present, and future. Although the kingdom of God has entered into history, it will not be fully realized until the end of the age, when all the kingdoms of this world become the possession of Christ (1 Cor. 15:24; Rev. 11:15). Thus it may be said that two phenomena are at work at the same time: the Church, the body of Christ, and the larger entity, the kingdom of God. The kingdom of God has been seen and manifested at all times, more or less hidden, but always there. The Church, on the other hand, is a mystery revealed in the New Testament but certainly not discussed in depth didactically or even prophetically in the Old Testament (Col. 1:26).

There are many who think that the Church in the New Testament takes the place of Israel in the Old Testament, that the fulfillment of the Old Testament promises and prophecies concerning Israel are spiritually fulfilled in the New Testament Church. These people generally do not see any particular future for Israel as a people and do not look for the literal fulfillment of Old Testament prophecies made in connection with Israel. But this viewpoint should not blind us to the fact that Romans 9-11 speaks about God's continuing concern for his people even in their unbelief, and the fact that before the consummation of the age many Jews will turn to Jesus Christ as their Messiah-Saviour. Nor should we overlook the fact that the Jew is back in the land of Palestine as a national entity. It would be difficult to label this as insignificant and would do serious injustice to the Old Testament prophetic utterances about the regathering of Israel from the ends of the earth (Amos 9:11 ff.; Lk. 21:24).

The Church as we know it had its historical beginning at Pentecost, at which time the Holy Spirit came down from heaven (Acts 2). Created by God through the death of Christ on Calvary, the Church was to be sustained and empowered by the Holy Spirit. This is why the Church age may be called the age of the Holy Spirit. The disciples were commanded by Jesus to tarry in Jerusalem until they were endued with this power. Jesus himself tarried forty days on earth before he ascended into heaven. The purpose of this was twofold: first, the disciples by repeated appearances of the risen Lord, his eating with them, and their touching him, were given all the evidence they needed to assure them that this same Jesus who had been buried in a tomb was risen from the dead (1 Cor. 15:5 ff.). The importance of this cannot be overstated. The most cursory reading of the Acts of the Apostles shows that wherever the disciples preached they bore witness to the resurrection of Jesus (Acts 1:22; 2:31; 4:2; 4:33; 17:18; 23:6; 24:21). This was the great touchstone of the Christian faith—no resurrection, no salvation. A dead Jesus meant a dead faith. But a risen Lord meant a real faith, a living faith (1 Cor. 15:12 ff.). The certainty of the resurrection was, for the apostles, based on what their eyes had seen, their hands had handled, even Jesus himself. It was for them an historical event like any other event in history.

The second reason Jesus tarried forty days was to instruct them more perfectly in the faith. He made real to them things they previously had not understood (Lk. 24:13 ff.). For instance, they had been told that if he did not go away the Holy Spirit could not come. Jesus taught them that they needed a spiritual power they did not have before going out to witness to and preach his resurrection. Only the Holy Spirit could give this to them. They were to tarry (wait) until they received the power (Lk. 24:49). There is a great lesson to be learned by every Christian from Jesus' command to the disciples. If those who were eyewitness to his resurrection needed this power, how much more do we, who were not eye witnesses and have not had the personal experience of seeing and touching the risen Lord.

For ten days the 120 were gathered together in the upper room, waiting expectantly in prayer for what Jesus had promised. On the day of Pentecost the Spirit came. There was the sound of a mighty rushing wind carrying everything before it. There were the cloven tongues as of fire, by which the disciples were enabled to speak in languages they did not know. All around Jerusalem men from various parts of the Roman Empire heard in their own tongues about the wonderful works of God. So the Church was born. The Holy Spirit having come, his ministry was to seal every new believer, to take up his abode in their hearts, to lead them into all truth, and to guide them every step of this pilgrim journey. He gave them the power they needed, the power without which their ministry could not have succeeded. The Spirit of God supplied the infant Church what it needed to survive and to fulfill its mission for Jesus Christ.

Jesus sent his Church into the world. The Church may be said to be both visible and invisible. The invisible Church comprises those born of God in all ages (past, present, and future), whose names are written in heaven in the Lamb's book of life. Only God knows who these are, for only God truly knows the hearts of men. No one can know finally about anyone else other than himself. Some who appear to have made a credible outward profession of faith, the only basis on which men can judge, may be unbelievers. Some whom we think are not in the true Church may be. God knows his own, of this we can be sure.

There is also the visible, empirical Church of Jesus Christ on earth. In this visible Church there are true and false believers, those who are saved and those who are lost. The righteous and the unrighteous will remain together within the visible Church until the angels of God separate them at the return of Christ (Matt. 25:31 ff.).

God did not leave his visible Church without means to protect itself against unbelievers and apostates. The purity of the Church as well as the peace of the Church are important. If those who disturb the peace of the Church should be rebuked, disciplined, and even disfellowshipped, is it not obvious that unbelievers and apostates who may be found in the Church should be excluded from its fellowship? The purity of the Church *is* important. Certainly unitarians in trinitarian churches should be rooted out, as should those who do not believe the truths essential to justification and regeneration.

The Apostle Paul went beyond false doctrine to include certain acts as worthy of disfellowshipping those who performed them. He specified that immorality, greed, idolatry, reviling, drunkenness, and thievery are sufficient cause to "drive out the wicked person from among you" (1 Cor. 5:10–13). The spiritual poverty and impotence of the Church

186

today are in no small measure due to its failure to follow the apostolic injunctions regarding church discipline. When discipline is lacking, the Church becomes like the world and thus ceases to be salt and light. When this happens the Church has ceased to be the Church. At that point true believers are required to withdraw from any church that professes to be a visible part of *the* Church, when in fact it has become apostate and thus no longer a true church. Let us make no mistake about it. When many of the Congregational churches of New England became unitarian churches in the great defection, they also became apostate. They became, and they still are, false churches by biblical standards. Once they denied that Jesus Christ is true God, no believer could be faithful to God's commandments and remain in such a fellowship (see 1 John 2).

We have said that God intended for the Church to be in the world but not of it. Why send the Church into the world? What should its ministry be? The Church has the unpleasant task of witnessing to the world that the judgment of God is upon it. This appears to be a dismal and a gloomy business; it carries no message of optimism, only one of pessimism so far as the world itself is concerned. The world does not want to hear such a message, preferring to be told instead that things are as they always have been and that they are bound to improve. They love to hear that men are gradually evolving into better people and that someday they will live in a perfect world. There are millions of non-Christians who are "good" people. They are often "moral" and "upright" citizens working for the improvement of society and the general betterment of their fellowmen. The perceptive ones are keenly aware of the many threats to the welfare of mankind, but do not realize that they have in mind the wrong things or that the devil himself is deceiving them in getting them to concentrate on secondary matters.

Many ecologists say the earth will become uninhabitable in a few decades; in thirty-seven years the world population will double its present size if the present two per cent annual rate of growth continues. Where will we put this multitude of people and how will we be able to keep them from polluting the earth through sheer numbers? Further, scientists tell us that man now has the capacity to kill off all human and animal life on the planet with nuclear devices. The overkill potential of these frightful weapons is such that the nations of the world have the power to accomplish this result many times over.

In the face of these genuine threats to an otherwise stable and inhabitable world, the pessimists of the non-Christian variety sound even more apocalyptic than the Christian. But their entire orientation and understanding of the threat differ from those of the Christian, for these well-intentioned people have a naive belief that man can and might destroy himself. The Christian does not believe this. God is still sovereign and continues to work out his own plan in history; he plans for the world to continue until he himself brings it to an end. Thus we do not need to fear that man will bring an end to history through self-extermination. God promised after the judgment of the flood that there should be seedtime and harvest, summer and winter, so long as time should last (Gen. 8:22). Man cannot destroy the earth. Only God can, and he will do so in his own time, at the end of the age.

What is strange about the non-Christian pessimist (there are, of course, millions of people who never think about these things or who are ever optimistic about the future) is that he does not seem to lose his faith in the ability of man to annihilate himself, nor see the incongruity of supposing that man can destroy this planet but that God cannot. Thus when the Christian brings his unalloyed message of ultimate and impending doom, the non-Christian either disregards this message or laughs at it. He has more faith in man than he has faith in God.

The message God has sent to the present world is not markedly different from the message he sent to Noah's world. Warning men that they would die unless they boarded the ark as their only hope for life, Noah's message was spurned. Apart from his own family, the world ignored the threat and paid the price of death. God sends a similar message to the world today via his Church: this world is passing away; it is marked off for final and irrevocable destruction; it's doom is sure. Now who wants to hear a message like that? Is it one of unrelieved hopelessness? Is there no bright light in the midst of this dark picture?

The Church's message is not simply one of unrestrained pessimism. Along with the eschatological note of a doomed world is the optimistic and bright hope that men do not need to perish with the world. The Church's message is therefore twofold: it warns men that the world is doomed; and it enjoins men to be prepared for the final judgment. This message of the final judgment offers hope to the hopeless, light to those in darkness. The hope comes through the preaching of the Gospel of redemption, which makes it possible for men to be saved from the doom and the wrath to come. The earth will not escape, but men can. The Church has its marching orders from the Captain of its salvation, who proclaimed: "All power (authority) is given unto me in heaven and in earth. Go ye therefore, and teach all nations, baptizing them in the name of the Father, and of the Son, and of the Holy Ghost: Teaching them to observe all things whatsoever I have commanded you: and, lo, I am with you always, even unto the end of the world" (Matt. 28:18-20).

There are three divisions to the Great Commission. Part one, the command to make disciples, has to do with the kerygma, or the proclamation. Disciples are made by preaching the death, burial, and resurrection of Jesus Christ; by urging men to repent and to receive him by faith, with the promise that they will receive the forgiveness of their sins, be justified before God, and be born into his kingdom. Part two of the Commission commands those who have professed saving faith, not simply in doctrine but in the person of Jesus Christ, to be baptized. This not only symbolizes the work of regeneration, but is the seal and sign of the new covenant of faith through the shed blood of Christ, even as circumcision was the seal and sign of the old covenant of faith through animal sacrifice. By baptism men are admitted to the fellowship of the Church and to participation in the ordinances, or sacraments.

The third part of the Great Commission has to do with the work of construction. New believers are to be built up in the holy faith until they have been conformed to the image of Jesus Christ. They are to be taught to observe all things Christ has commanded. Those who have been discipled are then called to join all other believers in fulfilling the Great Commission by taking the Gospel to all nations. The Scripture declares that Christ will not return until the stipulations of the Great Commission have been fulfilled; so long as he tarries we know there is work to be done, people to be reached, the Gospel to be preached.

I have said that the primary task of the Church is to preach the Gospel of the good news of personal salvation through Jesus Christ. This presupposes what was said earlier about the fall of Adam and the consequences of that fall. Man became estranged from God, was guilty, and had the penalty of death pronounced upon him. The good news is that in Jesus Christ anyone can be forgiven, have the guilt removed, and the penalty cancelled. But there are those who do not believe that evangelization is the true mission of the Church.

Hans-Ruedi Weber, the Associate Director of the Ecumenical Institute of the World Council of Churches defines the "primary task" of "the Church today" as "penetrating and transforming the world" (*Salty Christians*, New York, 1969, p. 9). If what he says is correct then it cannot be true that the primary task of the Church is to preach the good news of personal salvation from the guilt and the penalty of sin.

What Weber said is endorsed by men such as Professor James Cone of Union Theological Seminary in New York. He has defined salvation as liberation, "setting people free from economic, political and social bondage." Perhaps in a comprehensive sense one may say that ideally the notion of salvation *includes* this dimension; but this can be said only in an idealistic sense. For even if all the people in the world were to become Christians, there is still no likelihood that they would be set free from economic, political, and social bondage. The glory of the Gospel is that it sets them free from the guilt and penalty of sin, and repairs their broken relationship to God whether or not they are freed from economic, political, and social oppression. Even if all men were so freed those who lacked faith in Jesus Christ as Saviour would still be alienated from God and lost forever. Jesus himself clarified the issue: "For what shall it profit a man, if he gains the whole world and forfeits his life? Or what shall a man give in return for his life?" (Matt. 16:26).

That the chief business of the Church is to preach the Gospel is not the whole story, however. There is also the work of service. The Church is instructed to be a servant Church; even as it bears witness against the world, it is called to perform works of service to the world. This is the *diakonia* concept of the New Testament. This work of service is not a social gospel, although the Gospel has social implications and responsibilities. There is only one Gospel, that of the death, burial, and resurrection of Jesus.

The Gospel includes the call to men, whether to one person at a time or to masses of people, to be born again personally and individually. The service Christians render to the world may be a means to an end—i.e., to make possible the proclamation of the Gospel so that men will find eternal life. Or service may, in many instances, be an end in itself.

Christians, because they are Christians, reach out to help men everywhere. For years missionaries have been demonstrating this truth. Physicians have healed the sick as an act of compassion; they have also witnessed to their patients about Jesus Christ. But they have served the saved and the lost equally, because they needed help that the missionary could provide. Hospitals originated through Christian compassion; rescue missions in the large cities were established to lift men from the gutter and restore them to a life of usefulness; associations for the improvement of the conditions of the poor sprang from Christian hearts concerned with the impoverished. Wilberforce, out of sheer Christian compassion, successfully devoted his life to ending the slave trade. William Carey objected to the Hindu custom of immolating wives on the funeral pyres of their husbands; after years of patient effort he succeeded in getting this practice stopped. As a Christian humanist he had compassion which he expressed in action. Such concern and involvement was multiplied a thousand times in the history of the Christian Church. Christians are called upon to do these things for others even when they cannot, for one reason or another, verbalize their faith or bring a spoken witness. The Church is called both to witness and to serve.

The Church has still another function in connection with believers rather than the world. This is the *koinonia* function, the fellowship aspect of the Church. Believers are called together to worship God, eat at the Lord's Table, and baptize new converts. In all of these activities they are to be rightly related to one another. They are to fellowship to-gether—sharing one another's joys, sorrows, triumphs, and defeats. Here in openness they can bear one another's burdens and so fulfill the law of Christ (Gal. 6:2). It is true that God's people are sent into the world, but they must have a place to which they can go, removed from the world, so that they can do there what they cannot do in the world. Here, in the fellowship of the saints, with people of like faith, they worship God together. But it was never intended for the Church to become a coterie divorced from involve-ment in the world. Rather, it should be a retreat where saints regather their forces, recoup their energy and dynamic, and sally forth into the world again to spread the good news of the Gospel.

One of the great blunders of the day is the secularizing of the Church, the bringing of the world into the Church. This is a great mistake. It is right for the Church to be in the world; it is wrong for the world to be in the Church. A boat in water is good; that is what boats are for. However, water inside the boat causes it to sink. Here is the paradox —the Church *in* the world but not *of* the world; a Church that stoutly and vigorously refuses to let the world penetrate its sanctuary. This is virtually what happened in the Roman Catholic Church prior to the Reformation. Any cursory reading of the lives of the popes will reveal how wicked they were. Many were fornicators whose paramours and illegiti-mate children overflowed the papal properties. One pope was even murdered by the enraged husband of a woman with whom he was engaged in the act of adultery when slain.

Martin Luther posted his 95 Theses because he wanted to debate, among other things, the legitimacy and biblical basis for Tetzel's sale of indulgences, which promised men release from purgatory for sins they had not yet committed. Tetzel had taken a vow of poverty but in fact he was on salary, collecting money from ignorant and superstitious peasants under false pretenses, to help build bigger and more ornate churches. He also took the vow of chastity, but this didn't prevent him from fathering two illegitimate children.

The world is and always will be a problem and a temptation to the Church. Satan is the prince of this world, and the Church of Jesus Christ is his great adversary. Satan's business is to undo the work of the Church; one of the chief means at his disposal is to break down the barriers separating the Church from the world. Once the world gets into the Church its testimony is vitiated, its power is lost, its ministry is hindered, it stands in need of renewal. The Holy Spirit is quenched by the worldly Church.

The Church must have specific times to assemble apart from the world, so that the Church can be the Church. On such occasions the preaching of the Word of God should be directed toward believers. Somehow people have forgotten that the Church is the place where saints recharge their spiritual batteries and sally forth to do the work of evangelism among the lost. Therefore the chief business of the clergy should include preparing the laity to do the work of evangelism in the world; the clergy does this best by searching the hearts of God's people to make sure that all is well with them. Through the preaching of the Word of God they need to be brought under conviction of sin, make their confession to God, be filled afresh and anew with the power of the Holy Spirit. They need to hear what God has done through their fellow saints and how he has worked to convict and to convert sinners. God wants to purify his people, conform them to Jesus Christ, and energize them for battle with the world. This he does through the ministry of the Church to its own people.

The people of God are recovering a biblical truth that has been lost for a long time. I refer to a concept that had been described by some as "body life." Ours is a highly depersonalized age; people have become numbers. In the process, they have been psychologically and spiritually emasculated, suffering from loneliness, a sense of estrangement from their fellow believers. This has been due in no small measure to rapid sociological changes rooted in a technocratic, industrialized culture. Men and women work in large factories and offices. They are thrown together for a period of time each day, but their lives do not merge in any sense of totality. They live far apart from their fellow workers and see them only at the office or on the assembly line. They may eat with them during the lunch hour, but their relationships are shallow and less than fulfilling.

This truncated daily life is not improved on the home level. Multiplied numbers of people have become urbanized, living in huge skyscrapers and incarcerated in prison cells called apartments, from which they venture forth to work, shop, find amusement, go to church, and come home to watch TV and sleep. But apartment dwellers hardly know their next door neighbors and rarely meet those who live on different floors. The urban life is a form of captivity which is not significantly improved by flight to suburbia. Men and women spend hours commuting to work, only to come home to dinner, TV, and bed, with a repeat performance five days a week. Even in suburbia one hardly gets to know his neighbors except in the very immediate vicinity.

The body life concept is a good answer to the loneliness, depersonalization, and imprisonment of today's culture. In the local congregation men, women, and children can come together as members of the same body. The great truth of Scripture is that believers are related by blood, the blood of Christ, to every other believer. They are in the same family and are brothers and sisters in Jesus Christ. This new relationship in Jesus Christ is one that should bring people closer to one another than they are to their physical blood relatives. If all Christians do is come together for a worship service on Sunday and then depart for the rest of the week, the genius of "body life" is not at work. For this connotes a deeper and more intimate relationship of sharing, and openness about problems, victories, joys, and defeats. It is something that most churches know little or nothing about except in those, as yet rare, congregations where it is being practiced and shown to be effective. The practice of the body life principle in the local congregation will enable Christians to refuel and be strengthened to go out into the world to fulfill their role as witnesses to the Gospel.

The Church has the badge of love as one of its main characteristics. "Behold, how they love one another!" should be the standard response of the world as it looks on with amazement at the love displayed by the people of God for one another. By this shall all men know we are Jesus' disciples, that we love one another (see John 15:12, 17). Love must be based on truth. There is a vacuous kind of love talked about today that has little substance. When people chant "make love, not war," they are not talking about love in the biblical sense. This is eros not agapē love. When race hatred is manifested, as it is even by some so-called Christians, it is not this kind of love. Nor is it biblical love when those who claim to have it deny the great affirmations of the Christian faith. The love, agapē, that marks the Church is a spiritual love, refined, pure, devoted, and rooted in the person of Jesus Christ.

The Bible does not give any specific definition of love. How then can the Christian know what love is and when he has it? Paul came as close to defining love as any biblical writer, but only by spelling out love's characteristics. Thus one can know whether he has love if he possesses the characteristics that are common to love; whoever does not possess these characteristics does not have love. Love, says Paul, in 1 Corinthians 13, suffers long and is kind; love does not envy, is not puffed up, and does not act like a braggart. It does nothing that is unbecoming, does not seek anything for itself, is even-tempered, and does not think evil. Love does not rejoice when a brother falls. It rejoices in the truth. Those whose lives are characterized by these attributes have love. The Church of Jesus Christ should be filled with such people.

Now what is the relationship of the Church to the world? First we must speak of the relationship of the Church to the unseen world. It would be a mistake to suppose that all reality comprises only the things that are visible. Satan and the fallen angels have been discussed already. We repeat here what was said then: the battle between God and Satan is a cosmic struggle being waged in the total universe. It is being fought not only for the control of men and the planet earth but for the sun, the moon, and the stars of heaven. It is an invisible battle because God and Satan are spiritual beings.

Although the conflict is being waged by invisible forces, the visible planet earth is at the center of the drama. It is here that the plan of God to bring about the end of Satan's rule and power is being carried out. Jesus did not die on a cross on the moon, or Venus, or some other planet. He became incarnate on the earth; he died outside Jerusalem. The Church is central in the plan of God for the fulfillment of his purpose, his high and holy instrument to bring about the final victory and the downfall of Satan. Therefore the Church must be alert to the cosmic aspect of the struggle, the principalities and powers involved in it, and the nature of its own interest and participation. It is not called upon to sit in the stands and watch God and Satan fight it out on the turf below. It is summoned to fight, not to watch; to be in the arena, not in the bleachers. That is why men speak of the Church as the "Church Militant"—i.e., the Church at war with the powers of darkness and of hell. Some day it will be the "Church Triumphant," or the Church at rest. But not now.

Moreover, the Church in the world confronts the secular powers, whether democracies, dictatorships, or kingdoms. The Church is (or at least it should be) a rebuke and a threat to every government that does not rest on a biblical foundation, as well as a reproach to governments based upon a biblical foundation they do not live up to. It is dangerous indeed when secular states and the Church are linked together. God's kingdom and Caesar's kingdom are distinct; neither is to dominate the other, for the consequences in such cases are always evil.

The history of early Christianity illustrates what happens when Church and state are combined. During and immediately after the days of the apostles, the Church in the empire was persecuted by the Roman government. But the conversion of Constantine in the early fourth century produced an unexpected turn of events. The Roman Empire was "Christianized." This did not mean that all of the people in the empire became Christians; when the state became a so-called Christian state, however, Church and state were linked together. The end result was the decadence and ultimate apostasy of the Roman Catholic Church, which emerged as a result of Constantine's action.

During the middle ages the state-church combination reached a climax. The Roman Catholic Church became pre-eminent in Europe and claimed absolute sovereignty over state and church. The church was thought of as the sun and the state as the moon; even as the moon gets its light from the sun, so the state in this view derived its powers from the church. Emperors were crowned and uncrowned by the church. Henry IV was forced to stand barefoot in the snow at Canossa doing penance before the pope. The Roman church used the interdict and excommunication to keep both kings and subjects in line. It was such power that led to the Inquisition, to the loss of religious liberty, and to some of the most awful persecutions in the history of the Church.

If the subservience of the state to the Roman church was evil, there are other examples of how subservience of the church to the state produces evil as well. For example, Henry VIII of England wished to be rid of his queen, Catherine of Aragon, but the Roman church would not grant him an annulment (divorce was not possible under canon law). He therefore repudiated the Pope, who had named him "Defender of the Faith," and made himself "Supreme Head" of the Church in England. Thus began the Anglican communion, which has been the established church in Great Britain for four hundred years. The new, "independent" Anglican church was, however, subservient to Henry VIII and to a lesser degree to the kings who followed him; the Archbishop of Canterbury, the titular primate of the English church, was an appointee of the king. Henry's Anglican prelates knuckled under to him, closing their eyes to his many illicit marriages and murders. Blight eventually fell upon the church.

A contemporary illustration of a church that is subservient to the state is the Russian Orthodox Church in the Soviet Union. This church exists under a government that is atheistic and which has the power of life and death over it. We have said that one of the functions of the Church is to witness against the world and against sin and unbelief in governments. The Russian Orthodox Church does nothing to witness against the evils of atheistic Communism; its silence is thunderous. The Soviet administration tells the church what to do and the church does it. There is no religious freedom, despite the pretensions of the Soviet constitution that it exists. It is widely claimed, and probably true, that some of the leading churchmen are themselves Communists. The Russian Orthodox leadership is captive to these atheistic forces and has lost its spiritual power. If it were faithful to its Lord, and if it were to discharge its biblical mandate, it would have to pronounce judgment on the Soviet regime and take a stand for real religious freedom, not only for itself, but for the oppressed Baptists, Jews, and others who continue to suffer severe persecution at the hands of the Communists.

There are dictatorships that are not atheistic in which the churches nevertheless are subservient to political powers. Spain is a case in point. For years the Roman Catholic Church has served the political interests of General Franco. And there are well-known examples of a similar situation in some of the countries of Latin America.

The case of the democracies, however, is substantially different. In these countries the churches are free to operate as they please. In the United States the freedom of religion exists. Anybody can believe whatever he chooses, and he is free to propagate his beliefs; even atheists (witness Madelyn M. O'Hair) have the same rights. The danger to the churches in a democracy is not that they will be throttled by the state but that they may become so identified with the state as part of the establishment that they will cease to be a prophetic voice. Thus when the state violates the commandments of God the churches are tempted to be silent. God indeed calls his people to be good citizens of their countries, but citizenship in Caesar's kingdom takes second place to citizenship in God's kingdom. Therefore it is better for church and state to be separated, and for each to stay out of the other's business. But it is always the business of the Church to preach God's righteousness and to bear witness against the sins of governments and their rulers, as well as anyone else, when they transgress God's commandments. Adultery, lying, and stealing by a ruler are no different from the same sins committed by the least significant citizen. Both stand under the judgment of God, and the Church has no business to regard one person above another because of his high or exalted position.

To speak prophetically against the actions of individuals is one thing; to speak against the policies or the conduct of the state itself is another. A classic example of this problem came during the days of Adolf Hitler. With some honorable exceptions, scarcely any word of rebuke and condemnation came from the Roman Catholic Church or from the Protestants about Hitler's crimes against the Jews. The churches in Germany were generally tactfully silent about Hitler's government and its wickedness. There were individual Christians, such as Dietrich Bonhoeffer, who paid with their lives for their opposition to Hitler's policies, but the churches as a whole were silent. In a democracy, ministers, congregations, and entire churches can safely bear witness to their convictions about the policies of their government, so long as freedom of speech continues, and dissent is not punishable by imprisonment or death. Democracy makes it easier for the Church to be the Church. Dictatorships make it more difficult. In the Soviet Union dissenters end up in lunatic asylums or prisons. But the Church, wherever it is found and under whatever government, is called upon by its Lord to be faithful to death.

There are countries in which state and church are closely linked, with devastating consequences. In such cases the churches are so much a part of the establishment that public tax money is used to provide financial support for them. Citizens of these states are automatically baptized into the churches at birth, confirmed, married, and later buried by them as well. They may be active in their churches only on special occasions. When the state pays the way of any church serious difficulties inevitably arise. It is wrong to equate citizenship in the state with citizenship in God's kingdom. From a biblical perspective, it is also wrong to require people to pay taxes to support an established Christianity in which they do not believe. It remains to be demonstrated how Christianity can maintain its vitality and dynamic when churches and states are so closely knit together.

The Church is dynamically related to the kingdom of God. Its future destiny is part of this larger complex. What then is the destiny of the Church? In the New Testament the Church is described as the bride of the Lord Jesus Christ, a bride who is to be prepared for her bridegroom. Thus the ultimate destiny of the Church has to do with the world that is to come, a world that has already entered into history in embryonic form but which will be consummated when Christ comes for the wedding feast with his bride the Church. The Church is now getting ready to greet the bridegroom. Its eyes are fixed on the heavens from whence he shall come. For at his coming Satan will be dealt with, sin will cease, sorrow will vanish. And the kingdoms of this world shall become the kingdoms of our God and of his Christ.

However, until Christ comes, his bride the Church will be rent by schisms, torn by sin, and parts of it will become apostate. But Christ has promised that the gates of hell will not prevail against his true Church. As long as time shall last there will be a Church; as long as men inhabit this earth there will be a Church; as long as Satan is at work the Church will be at war; as long as any nation or people have yet to hear the Gospel the Church has a work to do;

as long as Jesus tarries the Church is the witness to his works, to his life, to his offer of salvation.

Someday the world as we know it will end. But the Church will live on—forever and ever, as the fellowship of the justified in the presence of the Redeemer, who is the King of kings and Lord of lords and who shall reign eternally.

XII. THE WORLD THAT IS AND THE WORLD THAT IS TO COME

The present world is under divine judgment. It is temporary and impermanent; it is passing away. This is the verdict of Scripture, not the verdict of man. The prophetic word of God sounds the alarm, warning men everywhere of the coming end of the world and the final day of judgment. Jesus spoke of another world that is yet to come, however, and assures all who follow him that they shall have eternal life in that permanent and imperishable city of God called the new Jerusalem (Matt. 19:29; Mark 10:30; Luke 18:30; Rev. 21:2).

In a number of eschatological passages (eschatology is the doctrine of the last things), Jesus talked about the end of this world. He explained the parable of the wheat and the tares to his disciples: "As therefore the tares are gathered and burned in the fire; so shall it be in the end of this world" (i.e., the consummation of the age) (Matt. 13:20). He reiterated the certainty of judgment, and talked of the separation of the just from the unjust and the end of the world. "So shall it be at the end of the world: the angels shall come forth, and sever the wicked from among the just" (Matt. 13:49). In the famous Olivet Discourse, Jesus' disciples asked him, "When shall these things be? and what shall be the sign of thy coming, and of the end of the world?" (Matt. 24:3). Jesus responded by foretelling the end of the age, saying that the day of the event is not known to men or angels, but that men are to watch and be ready so as not to be overtaken by surprise.

The Bible has much to say about the end of the world, and the attitude and the outlook of the Christian should be in harmony with it. The individual enters this world for only a short season and is no more; he brings nothing into it and leaves in the same condition he came in—empty-handed. Therefore, the Christian, having no enduring title to anything in this world, should regard material things lightly. For him the world is a place of change and decay, impermanent and insecure. Today's tycoon may be tomorrow's pauper; many political leaders are soon forgotten. The grave gobbles up all men's hopes of immortality on this planet, leaving in the books of history mere vestiges of what a few men said and did.

Moreover, every Christian should understand that this world always will be transitory and imperfect. At all times, in all societies and cultures, people have suffered, bled, and died. The dearest hopes and fondest dreams of the greatest idealists have never been realized and never will be, apart from God. Of all people, the Christian should be characterized by a biblical realism. This necessitates a utopian outlook, an anticipation of a golden age of glory, beauty, peace, and perfection. But this is an eschatological hope, the dream of a world that is to come, not of the present world. The believer entertains no illusory expectations that somehow this present world can or will become perfect. Sin makes utopia impossible.

God, strangely enough, calls the Christian to a life of apparent paradox. God has informed him that this world lies in the clutch of Satan and is doomed. Yet he is called upon to strive to make this transitory world what it is not and what it will never be—an ideal place in which to live. So the Christian labors mightily, knowing he will fail at last. He is encouraged by every sign of success against the power of Satan. Although the Christian statesman works to make this a better world, he is not deceived into thinking that his efforts will change the real direction of the world toward God. When bad governments are replaced by good ones, it only takes a decade or two before they become corrupt again. When crime is curbed by new laws, fresh ways are found to break them. Men of one generation swear that war has ended forever, but the next generation forgets what their fathers taught them and repeats the follies they committed.

The Christian should not yield to alarm or discouragement at the realization of what this world is really like. He knows he is a pilgrim, a stranger with no enduring citizenship in this world. In what then does he have hope, and toward what does he look? Because his citizenship is in heaven, he obviously waits for the Saviour. Just as Abraham acknowledged that he was a pilgrim, so the believer looks "for a city which hath foundations, whose builder and maker is God" (Heb. 11:10). Does this signify that the believer is to leave the world? By no means. But it does indicate that his attitude toward it will be quite different from that of the worldling. As Jacques Ellul has said in his book *Fausse Presence au Monde Moderne* (Paris: Desclée de Brouwer, 1966, p. 42), "It is necessary to mix with the world, but rigorously to refuse to lose oneself in it, and to preserve the specificity and the uniqueness of the truth revealed in Christ and of the new life which we receive from Him. It is our task to bring the savor of Salvation, of the truth, of the liberty, of the love which is in Christ, and never to allow oneself to be won over by the lostness of the world with its power, its splendor, its efficiency."

While the Christian labors through this life, he must fix his eyes on Jesus Christ. Caught up in the power of the transcendent Christ, his eyes do not waver and he is not drawn away by the lust of this world. Christ becomes his life, giving meaning and hope to the believer. This in turn gives purpose to life. The Christian does not simply wait dumbly for this life to end so that he can inherit immortality; instead he rejoices in this present life and accepts the challenge it affords to reflect the beauty of the Lord Jesus and to make his name known among all men. His is not a life of waiting but of service. In serving he finds fulfillment, and fulfillment makes life rich and free.

How does the Christian know that this present world is coming to an end? What will conditions be during the end times? He knows that Christ is coming again; Christ himself said, "I will come again, and receive you unto myself; that where I am, there ye may be also" (John 14:3). On the mount of the Ascension the angel told Jesus' disciples, "This same Jesus, which is taken up from you into heaven, shall so come in like manner as ye have seen him go into heaven" (Acts 1:11). Paul says, "The Lord Jesus shall be revealed from heaven with his mighty angels, in flaming fire taking vengeance on them that know not God, and that obey not the gospel of our Lord Jesus Christ; who shall be punished with everlasting destruction from the presence of the Lord, and from the glory of his power" (2 Thess. 1:7-9).

God has revealed what the conditions will be like during "the last days." On the one hand there will be wars and rumors of wars (Mt. 24:6; Mk. 13:7). Despite the hopes of some for universal peace there will be none; nation shall rise against nation and kingdom against kingdom (Mt. 24:7; Mk. 13:8). This does not mean that God's people should not work for peace or that there never will be evidences of peace as a consequence of their labors. It simply means that permanent peace will never come until the Prince of peace returns and puts down the powers of darkness.

There also will be famines, pestilences, and earthquakes (Lk. 21:11). In 1970 Peru experienced a great earthquake that killed thousands of people and brought famine and pestilence in its wake. Hundreds of live volcanos around the world can erupt at any moment. Tens of thousands of houses have been built over the San Andreas fault, which runs up and down the west coast of the United States; literally millions of people live on top of this earthquake area. Every geologist knows that sooner or later California will experience a great earthquake, quite possibly killing tens of thousands of people and doing billions of dollars worth of damage. Decades ago the city of Tokyo was destroyed by a great earthquake; today it has one of the world's densest and largest populations, and the probability of another quake is never remote.

The book of the Revelation foretells a time of cosmic disturbances, when the stars of heaven will fall, and when the sun will become black as sackcloth, and the moon become like blood. Kings and mighty men will hide in the dens and the rocks of the mountains, desiring the mountains and the rocks to fall on them that they may escape the wrath of the Lamb of God in the day of his vengeance (Rev. 6:12-17).

Paul teaches that in the end of the age apostasy will have infiltrated the Church. Apostasy differs from error and heresy, for men entertain error due to ignorance, and heresy may creep in as a result of Satan's snares; but these can co-exist in those who have true faith. Thus, for example, some believe in baptizing infants and others do not. Somebody must be wrong; whoever is entertains error but can still have a true saving faith. Apostates, however, fall into a different category. Departing from the faith, denying the Lord who bought them, they nevertheless often maintain formal connections with some church and outwardly profess Christianity. Paul says, "For the time will come when they will not endure sound doctrine; but after their own lusts shall they heap to themselves teachers, having itching ears; And they shall turn away their ears from the truth, and shall be turned unto fables: (2 Tim. 4:3, 4). Harold O. J. Brown says:

> The situation is such that one can speak of an anti-Christian mentality which has infected most of the institutions of the church, so that—again to cite Ellul —"Everything which drags the Christian faith through the mud and which tends to suppress the church is received with joy." . . . When prominent British critic and TV personality Malcolm Muggeridge became a Christian and wrote a book describing his spiritual pilgrimage, theology professor Harvey Cox wrote a review calling it "ill tempered and cranky . . . lacking in love, short on hope, and almost completely devoid of charity." We read that there shall be joy in heaven over one sinner who repents (Luke 15:7), but apparently none among fashionable theologians. . . . Nevertheless it is becoming increasingly evident that most theological faculties and a very substantial number of so-called theologians are a public mockery of the faith they ostensibly teach . . . it is clear that this represents more than mere academic freedom or radicalism: its proper name is apostasy. Perhaps nothing is gained by the introduction of such a sharp albeit accurate term; perhaps it would be better to carry on the whole discussion in an atmosphere of academic courtesy, never removing one's white gloves. But the courtesies are being discarded by another party, by the

frustrated students of theology in several countries who, tiring of the endless games of "atheistic theology" (as Klaus Bochmühl calls it), are demanding the substitution of Marx for Luther (Post- and Pre-Christianity," in *IFES Journal,* Vol. 23, No. 1, 1970, pp. 36-38).

There is apostasy in our day, and it will increase and abound before the second coming of the Lord Jesus Christ.

Jude describes apostates as filthy dreamers who have gone the way of Cain, have run after the error of Balaam, and perished in the rebellion of Korah. They are called spots in the feasts of charity, clouds without water, trees without fruit, raging waves of the sea, and complainers (vs. 5 ff.).

Paul also describes the perilous times and the general characteristics of men in the last days: they shall be lovers of themselves, "covetous, boasters, proud, blasphemers, disobedient to parents, unthankful, unholy, without natural affection, truce breakers, false accusers, incontinent, fierce, despisers of those that are good, traitors, heady, highminded, lovers of pleasure more than lovers of God; having a form of godliness, but denying the power thereof. . . . they. . . . creep into houses, and lead captive silly women laden with sins, led away with divers lusts, ever learning, and never able to come to the knowledge of the truth. . . . men of corrupt minds, reprobate concerning the faith" (2 Tim. 3:1-8). No one can look very far without discovering that Paul has penned a fairly accurate description of many people of our day. The end of the age will manifest these qualities in worse ways than has been done so far. This is why the Christian does not for a moment believe that men are getting better or that a golden age is around the corner. For the people of God these developments should not be looked upon as a misfortune, although they will suffer grievously.

Rather, they should regard them as a sign of hope por-
tending the soon return of the Lord. They are to look up,
for their redemption draws near—indeed, it may be nearer
than men think!

Those who know God and Jesus Christ will encounter
fierce persecution before the second advent. Jesus warned
about a time before his return known as the great tribulation, and advised his people not to bother about taking
things with them when they have to flee, not even to return
for clothes. They are to pray that their flight not be in winter, and if the time were not shortened "there should no
flesh be saved; but for the elect's sake those days shall be
shortened." He graphically portrays the horror, "For then
shall be great tribulation, such as was not since the beginning
of the world to this time, no, nor ever shall be" (Matt.
24:21, 22). Paul speaks of a "falling away" and of the
"man of sin" who "sitteth in the temple of God, shewing
himself that he is God" (2 Thess. 2:4).

Of great interest to Bible students are the political, religious, and economic developments that Scripture prophesies will come to pass before the return of Christ. In Revelation, John pictures two beasts, one rising out of the sea
and the other out of the earth, which are associated with
political and ecclesiastical power. The beast out of the sea
is likened to a leopard having feet like a bear, a mouth like
a lion, seven heads, and ten horns. Prophetic specialists
have developed a variety of detailed interpretations to explain the meanings of all of the figures. Suffice it to say
that the beast from the sea is a great world ruler having
worldwide political power which is given to him by the
second beast. The question is posed: "Who is like unto the
beast? Who is able to make war with him?" (Rev. 13:1-8).
He is all-powerful, a speaker of great things and blas-
phemies. His length of time is 42 months, or 3½ years,
during which time he makes war with the saints and over-

comes them. So great is his power and dominion over this present evil world that "all that dwell upon the earth shall worship him, whose names are not written in the book of life of the Lamb slain from the foundation of the world" (Rev. 13:8). This scene portrays a world gone mad, a world dominated and controlled by the agent of Satan himself. This is no picture of a lovely society, ruled over by good men displaying humanistic concern for the needs of men; it is a brutal and militaristic dictatorship headed by a man whom the Bible pictures as a beast, who is ugly, malicious, wicked, and hostile to everything good and to all that God and Jesus Christ stand for.

The beast who rises from the sea receives help from, and has community with, a second beast who rises from the earth. This second beast has all the power of the first beast, has the appearance of a lamb, and speaks like a dragon. He uses this power to make men worship the first beast, who has been miraculously healed of a deadly wound. The second beast performs miracles in the sight of men, who are deceived by them. He has an image of the first beast made to which he imparts life, and whoever refuses to worship the image is killed. His mark is a number, 666, which men must wear on their right hands or foreheads, and without which they can neither buy nor sell. The beast out of the earth is an ecclesiastical or religious figure; the beast out of the sea is a civil or political figure. The two beasts together form a partnership of evil (see Rev. 13:11-18). Elsewhere in Scripture we are supplied with information about this beast from the earth. He is the Antichrist, the counterfeit to Jesus Christ described by Paul to the Thessalonian church. He is also the false prophet of Revelation 16:13; 19:20; 20:10. He is the lawless one—not without law, but a law unto himself, and opposed to the law of God. He is called the son of perdition, whose "coming is after the working of Satan with all power and signs and lying wonders." God himself sends men a "strong delusion, that they should believe a lie" (2 Thess. 2:9, 11).

Thus at the end of the age power is concentrated in the hands of two men, one political and one religious, who, under the domination and incentive of Satan, are cruel and wicked tyrants. Under them the people of God will experience, as we have already said, great persecution and much suffering; these are the perilous times spoken of by Paul in 2 Timothy. In such a world the true believer is called upon to remain steadfast, to be an overcomer, not to count his life dear unto himself. Jesus intimates, however, that this period of persecution will separate the men from the boys; at this time, when lawlessness shall abound, "the love of many shall wax cold" (Matt. 24:12). So great will be the persecution, so intense the pressures, that many will desert their first love. No doubt this is why, in his messages to the seven churches, Jesus calls for those who profess him to be overcomers, to repent and return to their first love; to act, live, and die as true followers of the Lamb.

The climax of history comes at the last great military campaign or battle to be fought on the plains of Megiddo in Palestine, and called in Scripture the battle of Armageddon. Scripture does not supply the full details, but a general outline is given so that the people of God may not be caught unprepared. The Bible warns that Jesus comes as a thief in the night, at a time when least expected; yet Paul assures the brethren, "Ye are not in darkness, that that day should overtake you as a thief" (1 Thess. 5:4).

Clearly, the plan of God for the world, in a strange but wonderful fashion, involves the people of Israel. The Scriptures, the revelation of God in the Old and New Testaments, relate Israel to the climactic events of the last days just prior to the second coming of Christ. Paul in Romans 9-11 says that even though the Gentiles are branches that have been grafted into the olive tree because of Israel's unbelief,

God has not forgotten his people. The Battle of Armageddon will involve them, and the city of Jerusalem will have a significant role to play. In the Old Testament, Zechariah foretells the day of the Lord when God "will gather all nations against Jerusalem to battle" (Zech. 14:2). At the coming of the Lord, the Mount of Olives will be split in two, apparently by an earthquake. In the Olivet Discourse, Jesus said, "Jerusalem shall be trodden down of the Gentiles, until the times of the Gentiles be fulfilled"(Luke 21-24). Jesus' prophetic word was fulfilled in A.D.70 when the Roman legions under Titus and Vespasian destroyed the city. Josephus' account of the sacking is awe-inspiring. For two thousand years since then Jerusalem was under the sovereignty and control of Gentile powers; in the five-day war in 1967, however, the Israelis poured through the Mandelbaum Gate separating them from old Jerusalem. Now the city is once again in Jewish hands for the first time since A.D. 70. Is this the fulfillment of the prophetic Scriptures? If so, and it is difficult to suppose that it isn't, then it would appear that the end times may be upon us when the beasts out of the sea and the earth will rise to form the final coalition prior to the consummation of the age.

As this is being written the United Arab Republic and Israel have been at war off and on for some time. This has occasioned much dispute as to what the attitude of Christians should be toward the contending parties. Many evangelicals are quite sympathetic toward Israel, especially because of its significance to the end of the age and the coming of the Lord. Egyptian Christians have felt the sting of this and have found it difficult to understand; at present no significant numbers of Jews are turning to Jesus as their Messiah.

The United States has a great stake strategically in what transpires in the Middle East, the survival of Israel being in accord with the national interest. The Christian as a United States citizen is concerned about the Middle East, not only from the standpoint of national interest, but also because of its decisive role in the coming of the Kingdom of God. It so happens that God's purposes and perspectives do not coincide with those of the nations of the world, including the United States. To identify the policies of any nation with the will of God is hazardous. The intervention of the Soviet Union on behalf of Egypt and the Arab world serves as a case in point. The Christian rightly believes that the judgment of God is on Communism because it is atheistic; thus it is easy for him to suppose that by fighting Communism he is doing the will of God and is engaged in a righteous cause. Since the Communist Soviet Union is backing the Arabs it appears quite Christian to some for the United States to back Israel. Sometimes, however, God uses more unrighteous nations to punish and judge those that are less unrighteous (cf. the book of Habakkuk on this point); although in the end the more unrighteous will be judged and punished also.

The larger perspective of God's purposes should be kept in mind. God is interested in the Egyptians just as much as he is the Israelis. The Jews have come to Israel in unbelief; they have not turned to their Messiah. Zionism is to be thought of not as a religious but as a political phenomenon. The prophetic Scriptures tell us that even as Israel in the latter days will turn to God so will Egypt. Isaiah says that in that day "the Lord shall be known to Egypt, and the Egyptians shall know the Lord" (19:21). "In that day shall Israel be the third with Egypt and with Assyria, even a blessing in the midst of the land: whom the Lord of hosts shall bless, saying, Blessed be Egypt my people, and Assyria the work of my hands, and Israel mine inheritance" (Isa. 19:24, 25). Isaiah the prophet foresaw the calamities that would befall Egypt, but he also saw the moment of blessing when all Egypt would turn to God.

Isaiah and other prophets speak of God regathering Israel from the four corners of the earth. One fascinating but enigmatic passage says that "the Lord shall set his hand again the second time to recover the remnant of his people." Later "the Lord shall utterly destroy the tongue of the Egyptian Sea; and with his mighty wind shall he shake his hand over the river, and shall smite it in the seven streams, and make men go over dryshod" (Isa. 11:11, 15). The tongue of the Egyptian Sea is the Gulf of Suez, and there has been no known fulfillment of this Scripture up to this point.

When the stage has been set and the nations assembled, the climactic battle signaling the end of the age will be fought. No one can afford to be dogmatic about the political and geographical details of this final conflict. What part the United States will have in it cannot be forecast from the Bible. It is easier to find a role for the Soviet Union than for some of the other great nations. However, just as history began in the Middle East, so history will be brought to its climax there.

Zechariah prophesies that Jerusalem shall become "a cup of trembling unto all the people round about, when they shall be in the siege both against Judah and against Jerusalem. . . . In that day shall the Lord defend the inhabitants of Jerusalem . . . and they shall look on me whom they have pierced, and they shall mourn for him, as one mourneth for his only son" (Zech. 12, *passim*). "I will gather all nations against Jerusalem to battle; and the city shall be taken, and the houses rifled, and the women ravished; and half of the city shall go forth into captivity, and the residue of the people shall not be cut off from the city. Then shall the Lord go forth, and fight against those nations, as when he fought in the day of battle. . . . And the Lord shall be king over all the earth: in that day shall there be one Lord, and his name one" (Zech. 14, *passim*).

The battle of Armageddon begins as a battle of nations but ends as a battle between Jesus Christ and the beast and the false prophet. John in his vision sees a white horse on whom is seated The Word of God clothed with vesture dipped in blood. His eyes are as a flame of fire and on his head are many crowns. Out of his mouth goes a sharp sword. This is the King of kings, the Lord of lords. "The beast, and the kings of the earth, and their armies, gathered together to make war against him that sat on the horse, and against his army" (Rev. 19:19) which had followed him from heaven. The armies of the world are defeated and the beast and the false prophet are cast into the lake of fire. An angel comes down from heaven with a key to the bottomless pit in his hand, lays hold of Satan, the dragon, the old serpent, whom he binds and casts into the bottomless pit for a thousand years.

Those who hold to the pre-millennial viewpoint understand the Scriptures to teach that Christ at this time establishes his kingdom of righteousness on earth for a thousand years. His is a rule of enforced righteousness when the Paradise lost in Eden is restored for a thousand years. At the end of this period Satan is released and goes out once more to deceive the nations. Those who succumb to Satan's deception are destroyed by fire from heaven, and Satan is then cast into the lake of fire to join the beast and the false prophet who are already there. There are some who do not think there will be a thousand year millennium but believe that the eternal age will be instituted immediately after the final judgment following the return of Christ. In either case there is a final judgment. The righteous dead will be raised to immortality and everlasting life; for them there is the believer's judgment of which we have already spoken.

The final judgment is that of the great white throne. Jesus Christ is the judge before whom are assembled the unredeemed of all ages (Rev. 20:11 ff.). This will be their last opportunity to argue their cases. Here the books are opened: the book of works, the book of memory, the book of life; those whose names are not found written in the Lamb's book of life shall be cast into the lake of fire. Every man shall witness to the rightness and the justice of Christ's final judgment; every mouth shall be stopped and God shall be glorified.

The cosmos itself, contaminated as it is by sin, will also experience the judgment of God. Peter says, "The heavens and the earth, which are now, by the same word are kept in store, reserved unto fire against the day of judgment and perdition of ungodly men . . . . the heavens shall pass away with a great noise, and the elements shall melt with fervent heat, the earth also and the works that are therein shall be burned up . . . . Looking for and hasting unto the coming of the day of God, wherein the heavens being on fire shall be dissolved, and the elements shall melt with fervent heat. Nevertheless we, according to his promise, look for new heavens and a new earth, wherein dwelleth righteousness. Wherefore, beloved, seeing that ye look for such things, be diligent that ye may be found of him in peace, without spot, and blameless" (2 Pet. 3, *passim*).

The last act in the long drama of redemption is now to be performed. The goal of God's plan of the ages is about to be reached. Contrary to what most people think, the saints of God do not have heaven for their eternal dwelling place nor do the unredeemed live in hell. The lake of fire is the final habitation of those who spurn the grace of God and refuse his offer of everlasting life. The new Jerusalem is the habitation of the righteous for endless ages.

The new Jerusalem is that great and holy city "descending out of heaven from God" (Rev. 21:10). It has no temple, for God and the Lamb are the temple. It needs no sun or moon; the glory of God lightens it. The gates of this city are never shut. The curse is gone, the tears have ceased to flow. Death is no more, disease has disappeared, sorrow has been replaced with joy, and God is all in all. The Son of God delivers up the kingdom to the Father. In ages past the Father made a covenant with his Son, who agreed to become flesh, dwell among men, die for their sins, and win back the world that had been lost to Satan through the fall. Now the covenant is fulfilled, the work is completed, the drama is ended. The curtain falls and all is well. God is in his heavens and all is right with his brave new world where righteousness dwells forever. To God be the glory now and evermore!